T0162327

Quack Policy
Abusing Science in the Cause of Paternalism

Quack Policy

Abusing Science in the Cause of Paternalism

JAMIE WHYTE

The Institute of Economic Affairs

First published in Great Britain in 2013 by
The Institute of Economic Affairs
2 Lord North Street
Westminster
London SW1P 3LB
in association with Profile Books Ltd

The mission of the Institute of Economic Affairs is to improve public understanding of the fundamental institutions of a free society, with particular reference to the role of markets in solving economic and social problems.

Copyright © The Institute of Economic Affairs 2013

The moral right of the author has been asserted.

All rights reserved. Without limiting the rights under copyright reserved above, no part of this publication may be reproduced, stored or introduced into a retrieval system, or transmitted, in any form or by any means (electronic, mechanical, photocopying, recording or otherwise), without the prior written permission of both the copyright owner and the publisher of this book.

A CIP catalogue record for this book is available from the British Library.

ISBN 978 0 255 36673 1
eISBN 978 0 255 36689 2

Many IEA publications are translated into languages other than English or are reprinted. Permission to translate or to reprint should be sought from the Director General at the address above.

Typeset in Stone by MacGuru Ltd
info@macguru.org.uk

CONTENTS

THE AUTHOR

Jamie Whyte is a management consultant, a fellow of the Institute of Economic Affairs and a senior fellow of the Adam Smith Institute. He has previously worked as a management consultant, as a foreign currency trader and as a philosophy lecturer at Cambridge University.

He is the author of *Crimes Against Logic* (McGraw Hill, Chicago, 2004), *A Load of Blair* (Corvo, London, 2005) and *Free Thoughts* (ASI, London, 2012). He is a frequent contributor of comment articles to newspapers, including the *Wall Street Journal*, *The Times*, the *Financial Times* and *City AM*. In 2006 he won the Bastiat Prize for Journalism and in 2010 he was runner-up.

FOREWORD

State regulation has become pervasive in Western economies. Across different sectors, economic activity is tightly constrained by government rules. The scope for entrepreneurship and innovation is severely limited, with negative implications for both liberty and the creation of wealth.

The rapid growth of regulation has arguably received far less attention than the long-term rise in taxation and public spending, perhaps because the effects are often less obvious and more difficult to quantify. Nevertheless, it is conceivable that the economic impact has been even more pernicious. While 'nanny state' restrictions on lifestyle freedoms are generally well known, the vast amount of often technical legislation imposed on different sectors is rarely discussed in major policy debates. Indeed, the sheer volume and complexity of regulation mean that in many instances only specialists in a particular industry are aware of its cost implications.

For a researcher in the field of environmental policy, the expansion of state intervention is most apparent through the implementation of the green agenda. By raising the cost of energy, transport, housing and numerous other goods and services, environmental taxes and regulations are now imposing immense burdens on households and businesses.

Policymakers argue, however, that such interventions are

beneficial. The overall benefits are said to outweigh the costs, and scientific evidence is provided to support this assertion. Comprehensive studies, written by renowned academic authorities and peer-reviewed by their esteemed colleagues, are deployed to demonstrate the merits of new restrictions. Laymen must defer to scientific authority and accept greater state control over their lives.

This monograph exposes the deficiencies of this 'evidence-based' approach to public policy. Four policy areas are examined: minimum alcohol pricing, passive smoking, global warming and happiness. In each case, the use of scientific evidence is shown to be deeply flawed.

The author, philosopher Jamie Whyte, identifies numerous fundamental problems with the 'evidence-based' policymaking process, ranging from basic errors to more complex methodological issues. And he exposes the self-interested behaviour of scientists who stand to improve their reputations and finances if governments engage their services in policy development. Experts may also have strong personal preferences for particular policies and indeed strong views on how they think other people should live. 'Evidence-based' policymaking thus provides a mechanism for academic elites to impose their own values on society as a whole.

The case for such intervention is shown to stand on very shaky foundations. As such, it is scandalous that politicians have been so willing to introduce draconian restrictions despite all the reasons to be distrustful of the evidence presented in support of new controls. If ignorance is the excuse, then this monograph is essential reading for those involved in the development of public policy.

Clearly a much higher degree of scepticism about 'scientific evidence' is desirable, not just among policymakers, but also among the general public and those who promote state regulation in the media. Empirical evidence must of course have an important role in policy formation, but there needs to be much greater awareness of its limitations.

RICHARD WELLINGS

Deputy Editorial Director,
Institute of Economic Affairs
May 2013

The views expressed in this monograph are, as in all IEA publications, those of the author and not those of the Institute (which has no corporate view), its managing trustees, Academic Advisory Council members or senior staff. With some exceptions, such as with the publication of lectures, all IEA monographs are blind-peer-reviewed by at least two academics or researchers who are experts in the field.

SUMMARY

- Politicians and lobbyists who promote new regulations and taxes typically claim to have science on their side. Scientific evidence shows that the actions they wish to discourage are harmful and that government intervention would reduce this harm. Yet much 'evidence-based policy' is grounded on poor scientific reasoning and even worse economics.

- Recent examples of flawed evidence-based policy include the proposal to introduce a minimum alcohol price, the ban on smoking in enclosed public spaces, measures to reduce greenhouse gas emissions and attempts to increase gross national happiness.

- A frequent error is to ignore the costs resulting from the policy. For example, minimum alcohol price plans do not consider the welfare losses associated with reduced consumption among recreational drinkers. The benefits of alcohol consumption, and hence the cost of reducing it, are simply ignored in the analysis.

- Evidence-based policy typically also fails to account for substitution effects, such as the way a minimum alcohol price would encourage consumers to purchase drinks in the shadow economy or adopt intoxicating alternatives to alcohol.

- The external costs of harmful activities are central to the arguments for state intervention but often cannot be calculated with any certainty. To estimate the external cost of carbon emissions, for example, we would need to know the subjective preferences of people around the world, and somehow weigh them against each other. We would also need to make assumptions about the preferences of people living many decades in the future.

- The predictions of theories that have not been tested, and are not entailed by well-known facts, do not warrant high levels of certainty. Those who insist on this are not 'anti-science', as they are often claimed to be. On the contrary, it is those who are willing to be convinced in the absence of predictive success who display an unscientific cast of mind.

- High levels of scientific doubt are often concealed as a result of 'noble-cause corruption'. Scientists may exaggerate levels of confidence in their findings if it promotes actions they happen to support. This problem is particularly acute in fields that have long been policy battlegrounds, such as climate, health and education. Many scientists entered such fields because they were already committed to a particular policy agenda.

- Scientists are also interested parties. They stand to gain from policy taking one direction rather than another and will be tempted to support the personally profitable policy direction. Public policy can create demand for their skills and hence drive up the rewards accruing to them. Scientists are natural supporters of policies that draw on their expertise and thus inclined to overstate the credibility and importance of their ideas.

- Expert practitioners in one field may be quite ignorant

of other fields, knowing little about either their theory or methods. 'Expertise slippage' is the tendency to defer to experts on matters which fall outside their area of expertise. Climate scientists, for example, are experts on hardly any of the issues that determine which climate polices are best. They have no special knowledge of how businesses will respond to taxes or the relative welfare costs of reduced growth.

- Paternalist policies promoted by experts and politicians show contempt for the actual preferences of the general public. People are forced to live according to values that they reject. For example, supporters of 'happiness policy' believe the state should coerce people to act against their preferences in ways that policymakers think will increase their wellbeing.

TABLES AND FIGURES

Quack Policy

Abusing Science in the Cause of Paternalism

1 INTRODUCTION

Should the law stop shops from selling cheap alcohol? Should it prevent smoking in pubs? Should emitting carbon be taxed? Should people be discouraged from working 'too much' by punitive income taxes?

Those who answer yes to these questions, and who promote other paternalistic policies, typically claim to have science on their side. Science tells us that the actions they wish to discourage are harmful and that their recommended prohibition or tax or compulsion would reduce this harm. They are doing no more than promoting 'evidence-based policy'.

Yet much of the policy that wears this honorific badge is based on poor scientific reasoning and even worse economics. The appeal to science is little more than rhetorical bluster. The slightest scrutiny of the alleged scientific case for the recommended prohibition, tax or compulsion exposes its intellectual bankruptcy.

Alas, even the slightest scrutiny of evidence-based policy recommendations is too irksome for most journalists and politicians. So the mere declaration that a policy is evidence-based suffices to convince them of its wisdom. Especially when the declaration is made by a professor or the head of some august body, such as the British Medical Association.

And from this first rhetorical victory, a second is easily earned.

Those who oppose the prohibitions, taxes or compulsions can be characterised as anti-science, as people whose laissez-faire policies are so misguided that they can be sustained only by denying scientifically established facts.

This monograph aims to make this rhetorical bluster less effective by exposing the characteristic errors that pollute the arguments of those who declare their favoured policies to be evidence-based. They are partial in their accounting for costs and benefits; they ignore substitution effects; they pretend that mathematical precision is evidence; they confound risk and uncertainty; and they exaggerate the certainty warranted by the available evidence. Having committed such errors, they obscure them with grandiose irrelevancies about peer-reviewed publication, consensus among scientists and the proclamations of official scientific committees.

'Evidence-based policy' is so typically ill judged that the term should become ironically pejorative, as 'sincere' has become after decades of hypocrisy from those who make a show of their sincerity. For this reason, and because inverted commas soon become tiresome, I shall not use them when talking about evidence-based policy. Readers will soon come to see that I do not mean anything laudatory by the expression, and that no one should.

I proceed by considering four examples of evidence-based policy in some detail. I examine the British government's new policy of imposing a minimum retail price on a unit of alcohol, the laws against smoking in enclosed public spaces, policies aimed at avoiding global warming and the new move towards making happiness the goal of public policy.

There are many more examples of wonky evidence-based

policy than these four. But their mistakes are remarkably similar. Once you see how things have gone wrong in these four cases, you will be able to see the errors involved in most evidence-based policy.

The monograph ends with a chapter on popular confusions about the notion of 'scientific authority'. Deference to those who know more than you do is perfectly sensible. But policy advocates try to get far too much mileage out of this fact. By exposing the systemic biases of experts and the common rhetorical trickery of those who appeal to expert opinion, I hope to encourage a healthy scepticism towards scientific authority in policy debates.

2 THE PRICE OF ALCOHOL

Many British people drink alcohol. Some of them sometimes get drunk and behave badly. And some drink so much alcohol over an extended period that their health suffers. They become fat and have heart problems or get cirrhosis of the liver or something similarly nasty. Some die before they otherwise would.

This makes some Britons wish others would drink less. And not just wish. Some lobby the government to do things that will stop people. Advocacy groups such as Alcohol Concern have for several years recommended an evidence-based policy that they believe would reduce alcohol consumption and thereby improve the welfare of society. They think the government should set a legal minimum price for a unit of alcohol – a unit being 10 millilitres. A typical glass of wine contains two units. The minimum price favoured by Alcohol Concern and many other advocates is 50 pence, so that a drink containing two units could not legally be sold for less than £1.

In 2010 the House of Lords Science and Technology Committee lamented the government's failure to adopt this exemplar of evidence-based policy.[1] And in February 2011, Professor Ian Gilmore, president of the Royal College of Physicians and chair of the Alcohol Health Alliance UK, pleaded with

---

1   See House of Lords Science and Technology Committee (2010: ch. 4).

the government to adopt this policy, which was also described as evidence-based.[2]

In April 2012 the government finally relented, except that it planned to set the minimum price for a unit of alcohol at 45 pence instead of 50 pence.[3]

This is indeed an exemplar of evidence-based policy. It displays two of its characteristic errors. The evidence relied upon fails to account for substitution effects: that is, for the way the minimum price will cause people to adopt intoxicating alternatives to regulated alcohol. And, more importantly, even if all the claims made about reduced health and behavioural problems were properly established, they would not suffice to justify the policy. For they are partial: the benefits of alcohol consumption and, hence, the cost of reducing it are simply ignored in the analysis.

Most evidence-based policies depend on these mistakes, which is why I start with this exemplar of them. By seeing where the minimum alcohol price goes wrong, readers will be able to identify the mistakes that motivate most policies of the same sort, such as banning cigarette advertising (most Western countries), banning the sale of sugary drinks in portions greater than 16 ounces (New York City) and taxing fatty food (Denmark).

Ignoring substitution effects

A thorough investigation of the minimum price policy was conducted by a research group at the University of Sheffield in 2008 (University of Sheffield, 2008). This is the research

---

2 See, for example, Hawkey et al. (2011).
3 At the time of writing, it is not clear whether the proposal will be implemented, owing to opposition within the Cabinet and possible conflict with EU law.

that Alcohol Concern often cites as the basis for its support of minimum alcohol prices and which many of its other advocates ultimately rely upon. It is, if unwittingly, the basis of the government's proposals.

The results of the study are estimates of the reduction in alcohol-related harms that would result from various minimum prices for a unit of alcohol, ranging from 15p to 70p. A selection of these findings is shown in Table 1.

Table 1 **Cumulative discounted value of harm reduction over ten years**

Cost type	Value (£m) (50p)	Value (£m) (45p)	Percentage change (50p)	Percentage change (45p)
Healthcare	–1,373	–915	–9.0	–6.0
Crime	–413	–257	–2.4	–1.5
Absence	–238	–147	–3.3	–2.0
Unemployment	–5,402	–3,840	–25.3	–18.0
Total	–7,426	–5,159	–12.1	–8.4

These figures are derived by modelling the relationship between alcohol prices and alcohol consumption and the relationship between alcohol consumption and the harms in question (see Figure 1).

The monetary values in Table 1 are derived by multiplying the estimated reduction in the incidence of various harms, such as assault, by the cost of those harms, such as £27,000 for an assault with serious wounding. (I will not here explain how the cost of such harms is estimated, since it is not relevant to the argument below.)

To understand the mistake of this approach, imagine that instead we were trying to predict the effect of increasing the price

Figure 1 **From alcohol prices to alcohol harm**

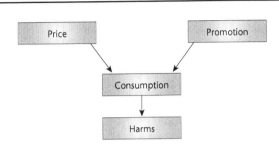

Source: University of Sheffield (2008: 30)

of air travel on public health. Aeroplanes sometimes crash and their exhaust fumes pollute the air, which contributes to respiratory disease and, perhaps, to a dangerous rise in temperatures (global warming). If air travel were more expensive, demand would fall and the number of flights would also fall. This would reduce the number of plane crashes and the amount of pollution from planes and, thus, reduce the harm they cause.

Suppose the *aeroplane-caused* harm avoided by a 5 per cent increase in airfares was worth £10 billion. It does not follow that a 5 per cent increase in fares would reduce harm by £10 billion. Because if people travel less by plane they will travel more by other kinds of transport, such as cars and trains. And cars and trains also sometimes crash and also pollute the air. To understand the public health effects of increasing airfares, we would need to understand such *substitution effects*. We get not only a decrease in plane crashes and pollution but an increase in car and train crashes and in car and train pollution. It is the *net effect* that should interest us.

The same goes for a study of the effects of minimum alcohol prices. People who respond to a minimum alcohol price by drinking less alcohol sold at regulated outlets are unlikely to change their behaviour in this respect alone. They are likely to substitute other kinds of consumption for the consumption that the minimum price makes them forgo.

One common response to increased prices is a shift to do-it-yourself (DIY). Just as minimum-wage laws mean that people perform much labour that they would otherwise buy from professionals, such as cooking and window cleaning, a minimum price for alcohol is likely to increase the amount of brewing, fermenting and distilling done at home. In Scandinavian countries where alcohol taxes are high, many more people make their own alcoholic drinks than in countries with lower alcohol taxes.

Other obvious alternatives to regulated alcohol include contraband alcohol and non-alcoholic intoxicants, such as cannabis, ecstasy, cocaine and the fumes of glue and petrol. There are also ways of getting more intoxication from any given amount of alcohol, which enthusiastic but cash-strapped young 'binge drinkers' may adopt, such as drinking on an empty stomach. Like drinking alcohol bought from regulated outlets, these substitute activities have health, crime and other costs, which we can therefore expect to increase if a minimum price for alcohol is introduced.

A study of the public health or other effects of a minimum price for alcohol that ignored these substitution effects would be worthless. We would have no idea if the net effect of the policy was to increase or decrease the harms considered.

Yet the Sheffield University study does ignore such substitution effects. It considers the way consumers will respond to a minimum price for alcohol by shifting consumption between beer, wine, spirits and alcopops bought from regulated outlets. This is included in its analysis of the price elasticity of alcohol consumption. But their model takes no account of how a minimum price would affect the consumption of substitutes acquired outside the regulated outlets.

So it is a mystery how the researchers felt able to draw their conclusions about the effects of a minimum alcohol price on health, crime, absentee rates and so on. If they do not know by how much a minimum alcohol price will increase the consumption of DIY alcohol, illegal drugs, glue fumes and the rest, they cannot know its effects on public health, crime and employment.

Publicly available data concerning substitute activities for drinking regulated alcohol are poor, if only because many of the substitutes are illegal. Even if the Sheffield University researchers had made a genuine attempt to capture the cost of the likely substitution effects, they would have lacked the data with which to do the job properly. Any number they came up with would effectively have been a guess.

The 'total' figure of Table 1, specifying a £7.5 billion reduction in harm caused by a 50p minimum price for alcohol, is correct in the sense that it is indeed the sum of the four numbers above it. But it carries no serious information. If a man takes two steps forward and two steps back every day for a week and then tells you that he has taken fourteen steps forward, he is not strictly lying but you are likely to be misled about how much progress he has made. That is no less true when he knows he has made some backward steps but has no idea how many. Having no knowledge of a number is different from knowing it is zero.

Ignoring or underestimating substitution effects is a

remarkably common failing of policies aimed at helping us with prohibitions or taxes – so common that it would probably be easier to list the exceptions than the examples. Nevertheless, it may be useful to give a few more examples of the mistake, if only to help readers anticipate where it is likely to arise.

After the Hatfield train crash of 2000, Railtrack, the firm that owned Britain's network of railway tracks, took the safety precaution of drastically lowering the speed at which trains were permitted to travel on large parts of the network. The increased journey times that this entailed caused many rail passengers to switch to travelling by car. Given that travelling by car is more dangerous than travelling by train, even at the non-reduced speed on the tracks of the time, this safety measure almost certainly caused a net increase in injury and death. Of course, the managers of Railtrack and of the Strategic Rail Authority, who supported the speed limits, were concerned not to save lives in general but to avoid deaths on trains. So the policy may have been a sensible means to their ends. But it did not improve travel safety, which was its advertised purpose.

Seeking to improve the diets of its pupils, a school in Northamptonshire banished vending machines in 2006. William Guntrip, an enterprising thirteen-year-old pupil of the school, spotted the profit opportunity this created. He started buying large quantities of sweets and soft drinks and resold them in the playground, making a profit of £50 a day.[4] Banishing vending machines probably led to a net reduction in the pupils' consumption of junk food. But given young Guntrip's unanticipated response, the reduction was smaller than the headmaster might

---

4   'School bans boy's snack empire', *Metro*, 4 July 2006.

have anticipated and not among the target pupils. Those who were keenest on junk food and ate the most were also most likely to use the alternative source.

This is a nice illustration of 'irrepressible markets'.[5] Prohibitions typically cause unregulated or 'black' markets to emerge. The black markets in recreational drugs and prostitution that arise wherever they are banned are the most obvious examples. But taxes and other kinds of price manipulation also give rise to black markets. For example, the taxes on cigarettes in the United Kingdom (about 80 per cent of the retail price) have led to a large black market in cigarettes. By various estimates, between 10 and 25 per cent of cigarettes smoked in the UK are bought in the black market.[6]

A digression on the patina of mathematical rigour

The Sheffield University study ignores the substitution effects of a minimum alcohol price. Insofar as its findings are taken to give estimates of the policy's net effects on health costs, employment costs and the rest, they are almost certainly wrong.

Even the estimates of the direct effects – that is, the reduction in harms caused by reduced consumption of regulated alcohol – are uncertain because, as the report admits, the data relied upon are partial or unreliable in various respects. For example, much of the data is self-reported, coming from the General Household Survey and Expenditure Food Survey. And self-reported data

5   This expression was coined by Mancur Olson (2000).
6   For obvious reasons, statistics concerning illegal activities are unreliable. Estimates are made by HM Excise and Duty and by the tobacco industry. The former's estimates tend to be at the lower end of the range and the latter's at the higher.

about 'personal' conduct, such as alcohol consumption, is notoriously unreliable. Moreover, the various data sets relied upon, concerning purchase prices paid and alcohol consumption levels, for example, do not overlap: that is, the samples do not include the same people surveyed over the same periods of time.

Yet someone reading the report might soon forget that the study followed a method and relied on data that rendered it incapable of producing numbers that should be taken seriously. For the data is analysed using the techniques of advanced statistics and the findings are listed in large tables and often expressed to four decimal places. For example, we are told that, for low-priced wine bought 'off-trade', the price elasticity is –0.4127: that is, a 1 per cent increase in the price of such wine will cause a 0.4127 per cent reduction in the demand for it.

Politicians and lobbyists at Alcohol Concern might be inclined to take these displays of mathematical rigour as evidence that the findings are reliable, that the study involves no gross methodological errors and that £7.5 billion really is the value of the reduction in harm that could be expected from establishing a 50p minimum unit price for alcohol. Yet they are nothing of the sort. Mathematically rigorous methods can be applied to any data, however poor, and can be displayed in work that makes profound methodological errors.

There need be nothing culpable in it. Researchers should always apply the proper maths to their data, if only to make the best of what little is available. And showing off advanced statistical methods need not be a conscious ploy to distract readers from more basic mistakes, such as ignoring substitution effects. But, intended or not, a patina of mathematical rigour does distract lay audiences from the errors that lie beneath.

This occurred at banks during the period leading up to the financial crisis of 2008. The board of a bank is responsible, among other things, for making sure that the bank is not taking unacceptable risks. To help them to perform this duty, they receive risk reports from their bank's risk division or finance division. These reports provide various measures of the quantity of risk being taken and the bank's capacity for absorbing losses arising from these risks without going out of business.

These figures are calculated by applying advanced statistical techniques to masses of data about price changes in tradable securities (such as stocks and bonds), borrower defaults and other threats to the bank's capital. Prior to the crisis, banks' board members knew that such 'rocket science' was used to prepare the risk reports they read. This not only deterred them from challenging the reports, since they had neither the time nor the mathematical ability to scrutinise the calculations, but also created a false sense of security. Few could have imagined that measurements derived in such mathematically sophisticated ways were in large part based on guesses.

This may also surprise readers, so I will give a simple and important example of a guess that underlies the quantities of risk calculated by the rocket scientists at banks.

Banks can suffer losses from many sources. Among other causes, borrowers might fail to repay their loans, interest rates or other market prices may move against the bank's position or a 'rogue' member of staff might make illicit trades that lose the bank hundreds of millions. Worse still, some of these losses may be correlated, so that the chance of one occurring increases if the other occurs. To know how much capital they must hold as a buffer against such losses, bankers need to know how risks are correlated.

For most risk factors – such as interest rates, borrower default rates and depositor withdrawals – there are plenty of data about correlations during normal conditions: that is, during non-crisis conditions. But this data is irrelevant. Banks need to know how these risk factors will simultaneously move during a period of extreme financial stress. That is when large, solvency-threatening losses are likely to occur. And risk factors that are uncorrelated during normal periods can be highly correlated during stress periods.

Alas, 'stressed correlations' cannot be observed in the available data because there have been too few periods of extreme stress. Whatever correlations are used in the rocket scientists' models, they will be based either on mere guesses or on irrelevant data (which is no better than guessing). Yet they have a material effect on the model's output: that is, on the quantity of capital it says the bank needs to hold. For example, shifting the correlation estimate for major risk factors from 0.10 to 0.25[7] could easily increase the capital requirement by 33 per cent, which, for large banks, amounts to several billion pounds. Despite all the mathematical rigour, the risk figures depend on guesswork. How many board members would have guessed?

This combination of guesses and mathematics told board members at every British and American bank that ended up getting bailed out in 2008 that their bank was massively over-capitalised. All of them had between 50 and 100 per cent more capital than the amount their risk divisions told them they needed to cover the risks they were taking. Given that most of these banks were leveraged over 35 times, meaning that a mere 3 per cent

---

7   Correlation ranges from 1 (perfectly correlated) to –1 (perfectly inversely correlated). If two things are completely uncorrelated, the correlation is 0.

devaluation in their assets would render them insolvent, this was extraordinarily implausible. Without the patina of mathematical rigour, the implausibility of the risk figures being presented to board members would surely have been more obvious to them.

Mathematical precision is a virtue in enquiry. But it is not the only virtue and it cannot compensate for other failings. There is no mathematical substitute for evidence. And, as we will see in the next section, knowing how to count is of little help when you do not know what to count.

Ignoring costs

Anyone reading Table 1 above or the Sheffield University report on minimum alcohol prices ought to be struck by an obvious question. If increasing the minimum price of alcohol has such large benefits – £5.2 billion at 45p and £7.5 billion at 50p – why stop there? According to the Sheffield University report, increasing the minimum price to 70p would be worth £16.2 billion. Why not press on, make the minimum price of alcohol £100 a unit and reap a benefit that will surely exceed £50 billion?

This evidence-based policy makes the same mistake as those who argue that the speed limit for cars should be reduced from 70 mph on motorways to, say, 60 mph, on the grounds that this would reduce accidents and save lives. Suppose it would. Why stop at 60 mph? Surely lowering the speed limit to 50 mph would save even more lives. Indeed, why not lower the limit to 5 mph, which might eliminate all road deaths?

The answer is that speed limits have costs as well as benefits. Lowering the speed limit to 5 mph on motorways would massively increase journey times. Travelling would cost more in time: that is, in lost opportunities to do other valuable things. People would travel less, and so interact with others less, both for business and pleasure. These costs would surely exceed the benefits of reducing the speed limit to 5 mph. This, presumably, is why the government allows people to drive, and occasionally to die, at higher speeds.

The same goes for the benefits that come from a minimum price for alcohol. They come at a cost: namely, the lost benefits that would have come from the drinking that no longer occurs on account of the minimum price.

As far as you can tell from reading the literature of Alcohol Concern or the Sheffield University report, there are no such costs to the policy. None are estimated and set against the supposed benefits. Yet the authors of these works must, somewhere in the backs of their minds, know that such costs exist. Why else do the Sheffield researchers restrict their analysis to a maximum minimum price of 70p? And why has the government proposed a minimum price of only 45p rather than 70p or £1 or £100? And, more obviously, if it had no upside, why do these politicians, lobbyists and researchers suppose people now do the drinking that their policy is intended to stop?

People enjoy drinking alcohol. They like the taste and they enjoy being drunk. You can tell they do because they are willing to bear the costs of it, such as the price, the hangovers, the ill-health, and the risk of alcoholism and its related problems. By reducing alcohol consumption, a minimum price will cause these benefits to be reduced. This is a cost of the policy. The size of this cost, when caused by a £100 minimum price for a unit of alcohol, will almost certainly exceed the benefits from reduced alcohol-related harm at that price. That, presumably, explains the government's failure to adopt this price. But how do they know the same is not true of their favoured 45p minimum price? Since the costs of the policy have simply been ignored in the research they depend on, they have no way of knowing.

The absurdity of this evidence-based policy can hardly be overstated. Imagine you were the chief executive of a furniture-retailing company. Your Head of Strategy comes to you recommending an expansion into Japan, claiming to have a brilliant piece of research to back it up. This is evidence-based strategy! You read the report to find that it consists of a mathematically elaborate prediction of the likely revenues to be earned from expanding into Japan (though it ignores revenues that will be lost from Japanese customers who now buy through your website).[8] You wonder what it will all cost. Will these probably overstated revenues more than cover the cost of the expansion? Alas, your Head of Strategy has failed to include costs in his reasoning. He is making his recommendation on the basis of the predicted revenues alone.

You would not only reject the proposal; you would fire your Head of Strategy for incompetence. Put in the same position with regard to alcohol policy, Britain's government hailed the proposal as brilliant thinking and adopted it.

Nor is this failing peculiar to the argument for a minimum alcohol price. Many lobbyists propose similar measures aimed at improving our health by reducing the number of calories we consume or cigarettes we smoke. For example, the Australian government has banned cigarette packaging that shows any image

8   Many business strategies go wrong by failing to anticipate such 'cannibalisation'. This is a similar mistake to failing to consider substitution effects when prohibiting or taxing something.

except a gangrenous foot, throat tumour or some other disease that smoking makes more probable. Branding is prohibited. As I write, the British government plans to adopt the same policy. It hopes this will reduce cigarette smoking.

Suppose it will. And suppose even that people's health will improve. How does the government know that the cost of losing the pleasures of smoking – the relaxation, the taste, looking cool or whatever it may be – does not exceed the health benefits? How do they know, in other words, that their measure will deliver a net benefit?

The short answer is that they do not. They have conducted no research into the matter. They have no serious argument but rely instead on a common tendency to confound what is good for you with what is good for your health. By showing (or claiming to show) that their policy will improve people's health, they assume themselves to have shown the policy to be good for people, as if health were the only good at stake.

But no one can seriously believe that health is the only good or that policies that drive up the cost of pleasurable but unhealthy activities generally benefit people. Many people trade off some health or risk serious injuries for the sake of pleasure. They eat foie gras, climb mountains, play rugby, have sex with strangers and so on. Increasing the cost of these activities, with minimum prices, taxes or prohibitions, cannot help those who now judge the benefits to be worth the cost.

Suppose Jack is willing to pay up to £80 for a certain pair of Nike trainers, and buys them because their price is £70. That gives him a 'consumer surplus' of £10. If the government applies a special 20 per cent tax to those trainers, so that their price rises to £84, Jack will no longer buy them, since he is willing to pay no more than £80. And his £10 consumer surplus will be lost. The tax will have made him £10 worse off.

The same goes when some of the price is paid with damaged health. Suppose Jack is willing to pay £3, plus a slight increase in his chance of ill-health, for the pleasure of drinking an alcopop. If he can get an alcopop for £2, he will buy it and receive a consumer surplus of £1. If the government sets a minimum price for the alcopop of £3.50 and Jack does not buy it, it makes him £1 worse off. The tax has caused him to forgo a £1 net benefit.

NICE is the UK's National Institute for Clinical Excellence.[9] A *Report to the NICE Public Health Programme Development Group* (University of Sheffield, 2009) explains that, although they understand that a minimum price policy entails such losses, they simply choose to ignore them:

> The public sector focus of NICE economic evaluations also excludes consideration of welfare losses (typically defined by consumer surplus – an economic measure of consumer satisfaction that is based on the difference between the price of a product and the price a consumer is willing to pay) arising from reduced consumption of alcohol. Hence consumer welfare analysis has not been undertaken as part of this study. (Ibid.: 57)

Suppose a university drinking society had conducted a cost–benefit study of the effects of subsidising alcoholic drinks, and reported that it would benefit society by £10 billion. Upon reading their report you discover that they have chosen to ignore the increased health costs. Why? Because they have a 'student party focus' that makes other matters irrelevant to them. No one would

---

9   Among other things, NICE makes recommendations to the government about what treatments should be available through the NHS.

for a moment think that adopting this 'focus' meant that there were, in fact, no health costs or that it justified ignoring them in a cost–benefit analysis. Yet we are supposed to believe that 'the public sector focus' of NICE either makes the consumer costs of taxing alcohol disappear or makes them irrelevant to a proper cost–benefit analysis.

It is nonsensical. Yet it is unavoidable for anyone who tries to estimate the net benefit of a policy aimed at reducing voluntary consumption. Unless you ignore at least some of the benefits of the consumption, you cannot 'discover' that reducing consumption would benefit people. For, as already noted, if someone is willing to bear the cost of consuming something, including the monetary price and any non-monetary costs, it must give him some benefit that exceeds this cost.

Of course, it is possible that a voluntary consumer has underestimated the cost or overestimated the benefits and that his consumption is net harmful. But it is difficult for a third party to judge when a consumer is making such mistakes. What appears to be over-consumption based on underestimation of the costs may in fact be optimal consumption based on an unusually strong liking for the consumption in question. Equally, what appears to a lobbyist to be optimally low consumption could be under-consumption based on ignorance of the upside. Someone who has never tasted red wine or experienced the intense physicality of a rugby scrum may be harming himself by living an excessively safe and healthy life. In other words, since consumers can make mistakes in both directions, the possibility of error is of no help to those who wish to push consumption either up or down.

Voluntary consumption may not deliver a net benefit to the

consumer in every case. But because third parties cannot know when consumers are making a mistake, nor in which direction, the default assumption must be that voluntary consumption delivers a net benefit, and that anyone who would systematically reduce or increase it is doing consumers harm.

This is why those embarking on research aimed at justifying policies that reduce voluntary consumption must ignore the benefits of that consumption and forget the general principle that voluntary consumption is beneficial to the consumer. If they did not, there would be no point even starting their research. Look at the research behind the policies aimed at improving our lives by reducing our voluntary consumption – be it of alcohol, fatty food or tobacco – and you will be sure to find this mistake.

But, once this mistake is made, the science employed in the analysis is redundant. All consumption has both costs and benefits. Provided consumers are not completely price-inelastic, consumption will decline if prices increase and the costs resulting from consumption will also decrease. We know this in advance of any research. So, if we choose to ignore the loss of benefits that also comes from reduced consumption, we know in advance the result we will get; we know the policy will appear to produce a benefit. There is no need to invest energy in working out precise price elasticities, the sensitivity of disease and crime to alcohol consumption, and so on. It is all a bluff. The moment researchers decided to ignore the lost benefits of alcohol consumption, their 'result' was assured.

External costs

Even if voluntary consumption benefits the consumer, it may

not benefit society because not all the costs of most consumption are borne by the consumer. In other words, some of the costs may be external. Consider kimchee, the Korean staple of garlicky fermented cabbage. I find it delicious and well worth its price, including the slightly elevated risk of bowel cancer that comes from eating spicy food. But there is another cost, borne not by me but by those around me: namely, my 'kimchee breath'. If we are adding up all of the costs and benefits of my eating kimchee, we need to include this 'external cost'. If this exceeds my consumer surplus from eating kimchee, then society – that is, everyone altogether, including me – would benefit if I refrained. A policy that pushed up the price of kimchee to the point where I refrained would make the world a better place.

The sum of voluntary consumption's internal costs and benefits – that is, the costs and benefits borne by the consumer – must deliver a net benefit (error aside: see above). So an evaluation of the benefit of reducing consumption must focus on the external costs. The internal costs have already been accounted for in the simple fact that the consumption occurs; we already know that they are less than the internal benefits. To know if the consumption should be made more expensive and hence less likely to occur, we need to know its external costs.

For example, just how much would people be willing to pay not to smell my kimchee breath? (Or, to put it the other way around, how much would I have to pay them to accept the smell without complaint?) Suppose it were 50p each for the four people who are likely to smell it. Then society benefits when I eat kimchee only if my consumer surplus exceeds £2. Imagine a bad breath tax of £2 were applied to the price of kimchee. Then I would buy and eat it only if doing so benefited society, only if I got more out of it than it cost everyone. The tax 'internalises' the external cost of my bad breath.[10]

Policy analysis might quite rightly examine the external costs of some voluntary consumption, perhaps with a view to setting a 'Pigouvian tax' that will internalise them.[11] In Chapter 3 we will look at an evidence-based policy that aims at reducing the external costs of smoking. But what matters here is that the evidence base for the minimum unit price for alcohol does not conform to this logic.

Many of the costs of drinking alcohol considered in the analysis of Sheffield University and NICE are internal, such as the reduction in 'quality adjusted life years' (QALYs). But, as already noted, these internal costs are already covered or offset by the internal benefits. So they should not be counted. Some costs considered are external but still not properly included in the analysis.

Consider, for example, the cost of crimes committed by the drunken, which are included in the calculation. These crimes impose external costs, whether they are committed by a drunk or a sober person. So, quite rightly, they are criminal offences even

10 This is not intended as an argument for taxing kimchee. Those who smell my breath are quite capable of returning the cost of my bad breath to me (and thus internalising it) by complaining or shunning me, neither of which I care for. The likely result is that I will brush my teeth after eating kimchee, as millions of Koreans do several times a day. This increases the cost of eating kimchee, but the cost is imposed directly by my concern for my fellows' welfare and their opinion of me, not by a government-imposed tax. As we will see in Chapter 3, external costs can often be internalised by such mechanisms, with no need for any 'policy', evidence-based or otherwise. And such spontaneous social mechanisms are usually more likely to impose the optimal 'tax' on externally costly consumption than a government is.

11 'Pigouvian tax' is named after the English economist Arthur Pigou (1877–1959), who advocated this method of internalising external costs.

when you are sober. Suppose now that the penalties for committing these crimes, multiplied by the probability of being caught and convicted, are sufficient to internalise this external cost.[12] For simplicity, assume the crime is grievous bodily harm (smashing a pint glass in someone's face, for example) and that the cost of the penalty is £50,000 – say, a 50 per cent chance of being convicted and suffering a penalty that you would pay £100,000 to avoid.

Now suppose that you are a bad drunk, the kind who gets violent, and that your chance of committing such an assault during an hour in company increases from 0.001 per cent when you are sober to 2 per cent when you are drunk. Then your chance of suffering the £50,000 cost of committing assault increases by 2 percentage points. This means that getting drunk costs you an extra £1,000. And the worse your disposition to violence when drunk, the greater this Pigouvian tax on your drinking. If your chance of smashing a glass in someone's face rose to 50 per cent, the tax would be £25,000, which would make drinking an even more expensive recreation than skiing.

In other words, the external cost of crime caused by alcohol is already internalised by the penalties for the crimes themselves. So the current level of alcohol-caused crime provides no reason to believe that the quantity of drinking now exceeds the social optimum. Just as the internal costs of drinking, such as ill-health, are already 'covered' by the internal benefits, so the crime-related external costs of drinking are already covered by the penalties for breaking the law.

The same goes for the cost of medical treatments that drinkers

---

12 By this logic, since the chance of conviction is always less than 1, the penalty for a crime should be worse than the suffering of the crime's victim. The Old Testament rule of 'an eye for an eye, a tooth for a tooth' was too lenient.

receive from the National Health Service. According to an NHS Confederation report (2010), alcohol costs the NHS about £5 billion a year.[13] Since the NHS is funded by taxpayers, this amounts to an external cost of drinking, borne by taxpayers. But this external cost has already been (more than) internalised by special taxes on alcohol which, according to HM Treasury (2010), raise £9 billion a year.

Internalising external costs *can* provide a rationale for taxing or otherwise pushing up the price of something. But that is not the reasoning behind the minimum unit alcohol price policy. Rather, it justifies the policy by calculating a benefit that counts the reduction in drinking's internal costs and external costs (some of which are already internalised) while ignoring the reduction in drinking's benefits.

Of course, many think people ought not to enjoy alcohol, and so ought not to feel any loss when something makes them drink less. But that is irrelevant. A businessman may think that the price of retail space in Tokyo ought not to be as high as it is. But if he ignores its real price when making his business plans, he is still making a mistake. And his business strategy, based on pretending the cost is zero, is certainly not the result of good, scientific reasoning.

The case for a minimum alcohol price policy really does depend on simply ignoring its costs. It is an ignorance-based policy.

---

13 The latest figures given were for 2006/07, when the cost was £2.7 billion. My figure of £5 billion was arrived at by applying the 85 per cent growth in this cost (in cash or nominal terms) that occurred in the five-year period prior to 2006/07.

3 PASSIVE SMOKING

You are allowed to smoke in England. Since July 2007, however, it has been illegal to allow people to smoke in your office, restaurant, bar or any other enclosed 'public' space.[1] The owner of an enclosed public space who allows someone to smoke in it may be fined up to £2,500. Similar laws have been introduced in many countries around the world.

This legal arrangement apparently takes proper account of the difference between internal and external costs (as discussed in Chapter 2). When you smoke, you harm yourself. That is properly your choice. You know better than anyone else whether the benefits of smoking are worth the costs, such as their price and the ill-effects on your health. But when you smoke in confined spaces where others are present, those others also inhale the smoke that comes from the end of your burning cigarette. And this 'passive smoking', as it is commonly known, harms them. In other words, smoking has external costs. These external costs are used to justify the ban on smoking in enclosed public spaces.

Like the minimum unit price for alcohol, this is considered an example of evidence-based policy. Many think it is justified by the science that shows passive smoking to be unhealthy. And those who dislike the policy often dispute the science.

---

1   Policymakers term offices, restaurants and bars 'public' spaces even when they are privately owned.

This is a mistake. Even if the science is correct – even if passive smoking really is bad for your health – this does not suffice to justify a ban on smoking in enclosed public spaces. Better outcomes would be achieved by leaving market mechanisms to determine where people do and do not smoke. The fact that an activity has external costs or unwelcome 'spillover effects' does not alone suffice to justify its regulation.

That is the central point of this chapter. However, I will begin with a brief discussion of the science of passive smoking – or, at least, of its presentation. For it displays two defects that sometimes occur in the arguments of those promoting evidence-based policy. They make the supposed virtue of their policy goal part of the argument about the science itself, and they fail to take proper account of the size of the effects they allege to require their recommended policy. But first, some preliminaries about testing hypotheses about cause and effect.

Testing the hypothesis that passive smoking causes cancer

How could you find out if passive smoking causes health problems? Ideally, you would take two large groups of people with the same characteristics (same mix of ages, sexes, races, health conditions and so on), get one of them to passively smoke and the other not, and then observe their health. If the group that passively smoked (the 'test group') had a higher rate of cancer than the group that did not (the 'control group'), then we could conclude that passive smoking causes cancer. Since there is no other difference between the groups, it must be passive smoking that explains the difference in their rates of lung cancer, heart disease and so on.

That's a simplification. It is possible that passive smoking does not cause cancer but that the passive smoking group still gets more cancer. Cancer could be to some extent random in whom it strikes and the passive smoking group could just have been unlucky. Or there could be predispositions to cancer that are unrelated to the characteristics in respect of which the groups are identical. And, by chance, the passive smoking group could have had more of these. So a positive result does not necessarily mean that passive smoking causes cancer; it does not *prove* it, by which I mean that it does not reduce the chance of error to zero.

But it does make it more believable. Such a positive result should increase our confidence in the hypothesis. Put roughly, our confidence should increase with the size of the samples and the size of the observed difference between their outcomes. Suppose that the experiment described above contained a control and test sample of a million people, that every passive smoker got lung cancer and that no non-passive smoker did. Then we should be very confident that passive smoking causes cancer. Now suppose that the samples contain only 10,000 people each and that the rate of cancer in the test sample (the passive smokers) is only 10 per cent higher than in the control group. Then we should be far less confident about the hypothesis. In these circumstances, the observed difference between the groups could well be the result of random differences between the samples.

Ten thousand may strike some readers as a large sample. We often read in the newspapers about the 'findings' of studies that have used samples with only a few dozen members. This is sometimes just a matter of shoddy science and shoddy journalism. But the required size of the samples also depends on the frequency of the relevant outcome in the relevant population. Lung cancer is very rare among non-smokers; about 0.3 per cent of non-smokers get lung cancer during their lives (0.2 per cent for men and 0.4 per cent for women). We should expect 30 people in a control sample of 10,000 to get lung cancer. A 10 per cent increased rate in the test sample would mean that 33 members get lung cancer. The difference between 30 cases and 33 could easily be the result of random factors. Imagine, instead, that the rate of cancer among non-smokers were 30 per cent and that the test sample showed a 10 per cent higher rate of cancer than the control sample: that is, 3,000 cases in the control sample and 3,300 in the test group. It is hard to believe that 300 extra cases in a population of only 10,000 is a random outcome.

A standard way of giving numeric expression to these ideas is to state the 'confidence interval' at which the null hypothesis – that is, the hypothesis that the suggested relationship does *not* exist – can be ruled out. The higher this confidence interval, the better the experiment supports the hypothesis.[2] As a matter of convention (following the work of the statistician Ronald Fisher (1890–1962)), experiments are taken to confirm hypotheses when they rule out the null hypothesis at the 95 per cent confidence interval: that is, when the probability that the result was a matter of chance is 5 per cent or less.

Alas, in the medical and social sciences, the kind of controlled experiment described above is often practically impossible. If a scientist suspects something is lethal, he will find it difficult – for reasons of law, commerce and, perhaps, conscience – to recruit experimental subjects to join the test group of his experiment. So social and medical scientists instead rely on 'natural experiments'.

A natural experiment can be performed when a population

2   Readers who would like to know how these confidence intervals are calculated can consult almost any textbook for statistics undergraduates.

'naturally' divides itself into a test group and a control group: that is, when the division is not the contrivance of the experimenters but has already occurred for some reason.

Consider, for example, the hypothesis that certain levels of exposure to ultra-violet light (UV) cause malignant melanomas (an often fatal kind of skin cancer). An ethical medical researcher is unlikely to perform a controlled experiment in which he exposes members of the test group to what he takes to be carcinogenic quantities of UV. But this does not prevent the hypothesis from being tested, because people naturally divide themselves into test and control groups.

For example, many white New Zealanders are of Scottish descent. Yet they are exposed to much higher levels of UV than Scots who live in Scotland. If Scots in New Zealand suffer higher rates of skin cancer than Scots in Scotland, as they do, this supports the hypothesis that UV causes skin cancer.

Of course, differing exposure to UV is unlikely to be the only difference between New Zealand Scots and Scottish Scots. For example, their diets may also differ, some Scots may use sunbeds and some New Zealanders may avoid sunburn by wearing hats and sunblock.

But it is not beyond the wit of natural experimenters to 'control for' such variations. That is, they can identify groups of New Zealand Scots and Scottish Scots with sufficiently similar diets and use of sunbeds and sunblock to construct proper test and control groups for the hypothesis in question. In this case, the easiest solution is to look at skin cancer rates from before 1980, when the diets of white New Zealanders and Scots were very similar, when almost no one, anywhere in the world, used sunbeds and when few New Zealanders used sunblock.

As with skin cancer and UV, evidence about the health effects of passive smoking is derived from natural rather than contrived experiments. Some non-smokers live with smokers and some do not. This provides the basis for a natural experiment. Is the health of non-smokers who live with smokers (the test group) worse than the health of those who do not (the control group)?

Of course, these passive smokers and complete non-smokers are unlikely to differ in this respect alone. For example, the passive smokers may be more inclined than the non-passive smokers to do other things, such as disregard supposed health risks, which accounts for their ill-health. For example, passive smokers may also drink heavily, eat lots of sweet food or take little exercise. And it may be one or more of these things, rather than the passive smoking, that accounts for any discovered difference in the health of the test and control groups.

But, as with the differences in diet between New Zealand Scots and Scottish Scots, this need not be an insuperable problem. The differing habits of passive smokers and passive non-smokers can be observed – or, at least, they can be reported by those who have them.[3] And this makes it possible to 'control for' such differences in behaviour: that is, to construct sufficiently similar test and control groups.

Several such natural experiments have been conducted over

3   Such reports are not wholly reliable because they involve behaviour that the self-reporter may wish to misrepresent. And, as a matter of fact, most of the natural experiments into the effects of passive smoking have not attempted to observe the other habits of the control and test groups to ensure that it is not one of these, rather than passive smoking, that may have caused any observed health differences. Or, in the terminology of statistical testing, they have not done enough to rule out the potential effects of confounding factors. But if we make no allowances for the science of passive smoking, it will be difficult to get to the really big mistakes in the evidence-based policy it is imagined to support.

recent decades. They have delivered different results. Some have failed to place the null hypothesis below the 5 per cent confidence interval. In other words, they have failed to provide the hypothesis that passive smoking causes lung cancer (and the rest of the alleged health problems) with the conventionally accepted degree of certainty. Others have confirmed the hypothesis. They have suggested that passive smoking increases the chance of contracting lung cancer by between 10 per cent and 50 per cent.

Because the results of individual studies vary so widely, with several indicating that passive smoking has no effect on health, the official opinion on the matter is typically based on 'meta-analyses'. A meta-analysis considers the findings of all the studies whose method is deemed to pass a threshold standard. Usually the methodological standard concerns data collection and the way in which the test and control samples were constructed. In the case of passive smoking, the difficulty lies in ensuring that people are properly allocated to the passive smoking and complete non-smoking groups. The non-smoking spouse of a smoker who is assigned to the test group may not in fact do much passive smoking, perhaps because his wife always smokes on the balcony. Or a non-smoker assigned to the control group, because he is married to a non-smoker, may in fact spend most nights of the week playing poker with his smoking friends. Studies vary in how strenuously they have attempted to ensure that such misclassifications do not occur.

Studies that pass the threshold for inclusion are then weighted according to their quality, which is primarily a matter of their method of data collection (see above) and their sample sizes. The result of a meta-analysis is the weighted average finding of the studies considered. A meta-analysis thus attempts to take account of all the reliable evidence that has been made available by the studies conducted.

Since the individual studies disagree in their findings, at best all but one of them are wrong. Alas, we do not know which of the studies included in the meta-analysis went wrong. If we did, they would not be included in the meta-analysis. This means it is more rational to believe the result of the meta-analysis than to believe the result of any one of its constituent studies.

Good science is bad science

In 1992, the US Environmental Protection Agency (EPA) published the results of such a meta-analysis (EPA, 1992). It declared that passive smoking or Environmental Tobacco Smoke (ETS), as the EPA calls it, increases your chance of getting lung cancer by 19 per cent, which entails 3,000 extra deaths a year in the USA.

The EPA arrived at this conclusion by considering 30 studies of passive smoking. Of these, only five found a statistically significant risk at the 95 per cent confidence interval. One study showed a protective effect of passive smoking and 24 found no effect either way. Under such circumstances, the discovery of a 19 per cent increased chance of cancer may seem surprising, even allowing for the increased sample size created by the meta-analysis. So it should. This result was achieved by eliminating all but eleven of the available studies from the meta-analysis and by using a 90 per cent rather than a 95 per cent confidence level for stating the result. At the 95 per cent confidence interval, the null hypothesis could not be ruled out – that is, the probability that the result was a matter of chance exceeded 5 per cent. But it did not exceed 10 per cent. So the EPA parted with scientific convention and used the lower 90 per cent standard to announce a positive finding.

Why did the EPA do this? Below is a passage from a 1993 *Wall Street Journal* article on the topic, which quotes the EPA's statistical consultant, Dr Wood:

> The EPA believes it is inconceivable that breathing in smoke containing known cancer-causing substances could be healthy and any hint in the report that it might be would be meaningless and confusing, he explains. 'I could have presented any level of confidence interval you wanted and it still wouldn't change the conclusion' that passive smoking boosts the risk of lung cancer an average of 19%, he says. 'The confidence interval isn't a substantive issue,' Mr. Wood says. The 90% confidence interval used in the report was added for the convenience of scientifically oriented readers. The tobacco industry's harping on it, he says, 'is just to confuse the public.'[4]

This passage suggests that the meta-analysis performed by EPA was not intended to test the hypothesis that passive smoking causes cancer. They were already convinced that it did – or, as Wood put it, the idea that it did not was 'inconceivable'. The purpose was to get the public to believe what the EPA already believed. And if this required lowering the conventional standards for statistical confirmation by doubling the margin of error (from 5 per cent to 10 per cent), then they were happy to do so. After all, they were simply trying to avoid saying things that would have been 'meaningless and confusing'. Under these circumstances, it is those who insist on applying the conventional standard of confirmation who were 'just trying to confuse the public'.

---

4 'Statisticians occupy front lines in battle over passive smoking', *Wall Street Journal*, 28 July 1993, p. B1.

This is a perfect example of 'noble-cause corruption', an expression initially coined to describe the illegal police practice of fabricating evidence to convict people who they believe to be guilty. More broadly, it means engaging in intellectual shenanigans for the sake of promoting a good cause, such as not 'confusing the public' about the dangers of passive smoking.

It is popular among politicians, who often misrepresent the strength of the evidence for the alleged facts they use to justify their policies. For example, Clare Short, the former International Development Secretary, accused Tony Blair of it when she described his exaggerated claims about the military threat posed by Iraq as an 'honourable deception'. And, as Dr Wood reminds us, scientists sometimes do it too.

I will not enter the debate about whether such lying is honourable or genuinely corrupt. It is not the ethics that should concern us but the absurdity. The case for evidence-based policies is supposed to depend on the strength of the evidence for the relevant hypothesis: for example, that passive smoking causes cancer. If you take the policy consequences of belief in the hypothesis to be part of the case for the hypothesis, then your reasoning is hopelessly circular. We should support the policy because it is based on evidence. And what is that evidence? That if we believe in the hypothesis, we will support the policy.

Scientists' intentions are irrelevant to standards of confirmation by evidence. A desire to improve people's health or otherwise 'do good' does not mean that your judgements about cause and effect are more likely to be true and hence in need of a less stringent evidential standard. There is no moral substitute for evidence. Equally, selfish or otherwise unsavoury motives do not increase the amount of evidence required by your hypotheses.

If a priest presents you with a new argument for the existence of God, you cannot properly dismiss it by pointing out that his income depends on people believing in God. The argument might still prove the existence of God. If you want to show that it does not, you will need to explain where its error lies, which cannot be the fact that the man presenting it benefits from its being correct. When assessing arguments or evidence for some conclusion, the motives of the person providing them are irrelevant.

Motives are relevant only when we are being asked to accept some hypothesis on someone's say so alone: that is, when we are dealing with testimony (see Chapter 6). If that priest offered no argument or evidence but just said, 'Trust me, I know God exists because I saw Him last week', his vested interest in the conclusion might properly make you doubt his reliability as a witness. But science does not deal in mere assertion or appeals to personal credibility; it deals in rigorous methods of testing hypotheses against publicly available or reproducible evidence. That is why the motives of scientists are never mentioned in a scientific debate.

Or, at least, it is why they never should be. In fact, they occasionally are. And the debate about passive smoking is one such occasion.

In 2003, James Enstrom and Geoffrey Kabat published a paper in the *British Medical Journal* (*BMJ*) reporting findings of a long-term study of passive smoking. It did not confirm the hypothesis that passive smoking causes serious disease. Even before the article was published, the American Cancer Society issued a press release stating that these findings were based on shoddy scientific practice. The *BMJ* has not retracted its publication of the article, as it does when it comes to believe articles are based on shoddy practice. Nevertheless, the study's findings are commonly excluded from the meta-analyses that allegedly confirm that passive smoking causes serious disease. The study has even been cited in the 2006 post-trial 'findings of fact' prepared by the US Department of Justice regarding a lawsuit brought by the US government against the tobacco firm Philip Morris in 1999. It is discussed in a section entitled 'Cooking the Books: the Manufacture of False Science to Support the [Tobacco] Industry position on ETS [Environmental Tobacco Smoke]'.

James Enstrom is busily trying to defend both his original *BMJ* paper and his reputation for scientific integrity. Anyone interested in trying to decide whether or not his *BMJ* paper meets the normal standards of research in this field can do so by reading the many critiques and defences to be found on the Internet. But that issue is not my current concern, if only because, as we will see below, it is irrelevant to the case for banning smoking in enclosed public spaces.

Rather, the notable fact about this controversy is that critics of Enstrom and Kabat's BMJ paper frequently claimed that their research was funded by tobacco firms. This was supposed to undermine the credibility of their findings. Since tobacco firms benefit if research shows no causal connection between passive smoking and disease, the findings of research funded by tobacco firms cannot be trusted. That is the line of reasoning.

Indeed, Professor Stanton Glantz, another medical scientist, was so concerned about this supposed problem that in 2007 he asked the University of California to introduce a rule requiring its academic staff to reject funding from tobacco firms.[5] (The

5   See, for example, 'Petition not to accept tobacco industry funding', http://senate.ucsf.edu/townhallmeeting/TobaccoPetition.PDF.

university rejected Glantz's proposal on grounds of intellectual freedom.)

Such fretting about the sources of scientists' funding is familiar. But it is strange, especially coming from scientists. Glantz's demand that University of California researchers never accept funding from tobacco companies displays a peculiar lack of confidence in the rigour of his own field of inquiry. If studies into the health effects of passive smoking can be conducted in a way that warrants belief in their conclusions, then extra funding of research can only advance our knowledge, regardless of where that funding comes from. Suppose the research funded by tobacco companies does not conform to the required standard. Then Glantz and his peers will be able to tell that it does not, and the findings can be set aside. Or suppose it does meet the required standard. Then Glantz should welcome the addition to the body of good research in the area. Either way, if the field Glantz works in has clear standards, he has nothing to fear from research funded by tobacco companies.

Yet Glantz and others do fear it. Indeed, they want it banned. This suggests that they lack confidence in the methods of their own field of research. They regard the statements of their colleagues as incapable of confirmation or refutation by evidence. When a 'scientist' tells us that passive smoking causes cancer, or that it does not, he is simply testifying. We cannot rely on the evidence but must instead make a judgement about his motivations for saying what he does.

If so, then we should doubt the findings not only of those who are funded by tobacco companies but of everyone working in the field. It is not a field of sufficient rigour to warrant our credence. A scientist who claims that a rival's credibility is undermined by his motives thereby undermines his own credibility.

A relatively large ant is still small

Does passive smoking cause cancer and other health problems, such as heart disease? Or, in other words, does passive smoking increase the chance that you will get cancer? (For simplicity, I shall henceforth omit reference to the other alleged harms of passive smoking – they can be added back in when we come to the reckoning.) The debate between Enstrom and Glantz concerns the certainty of the proposition that it does. For the sake of argument, suppose the matter were beyond doubt: passive smoking increases the chance of cancer. Nothing immediately follows about whether either legislators or passive smokers should care. As with any other harmful activity, how much you care about passive smoking should also depend on the size of the effect.

You might be shot while walking the streets. A bulletproof vest or body armour (as it is now known) would at least halve your chance of death should you be shot. Those not wearing one are doubling their chance of dying from a gunshot. Are they being foolish?

It depends, of course, on their chance of being shot. And this depends on where they are. War correspondents typically wear bulletproof vests; people shopping in Hampstead do not. The logic is simple. In Helmand Province, let's suppose, a reporter sent on a one-year assignment faces a 2 per cent annual chance of being shot and killed without a bulletproof vest and a 1 per cent chance of being shot and killed with it. Bulletproof vests cost about £1,000. Let's suppose they can be sold for £500 after the assignment. Then it is worth the expense of wearing one provided the journalist values a 1 per cent reduction in his annual chance of dying at more than £500. Which he may well do.

Now consider the shoppers of Hampstead. Their annual

chance of being shot is extraordinarily small, less than 1 in a million or 0.0001 per cent.[6] So wearing a bulletproof vest in Hampstead would require you to value a 0.00005 per cent reduction in your chance of death at £500. This exceeds even the self-worth of Hampstead shoppers, as can be observed from the lack of flak jackets in their wardrobes.

The amount people are willing to spend to reduce small probabilities of dying allows us to derive a 'value of a statistical life'. For example, suppose the average person is willing to spend £500 to reduce his chance of dying during the coming year by 1 per cent. This suggests that he values a statistical year's life at £50,000. If the average person lives 80 years, this implies a whole statistical life is worth £4 million.[7] Such statistical values of life are used by policymakers to decide how much to spend to reduce risks of death. Should the government spend £20 million to improve the safety of a stretch of motorway? The answer depends on how many lives are likely to be saved and what those statistical lives are worth. Only if the answer is greater than £20 million are the improvements worthwhile.

As the above examples show, how much we should care about a cause of some harm depends not only on the percentage by which it increases the chance of that harm but on what the chance was to begin with. In other words, we need to know the *absolute* increase in the chance.

---

6   To the best of my knowledge, only one person has been shot in Hampstead in the last 100 years, and hundreds of thousands pass through Hampstead every year.

7   In practice a person's valuation of a year's life is likely to vary over time. Note that the value of a statistical life is not the same as what someone would be willing to spend to avoid certain death. In most circumstances, people would be willing to spend much more than the value of a statistical life to avoid their own certain death.

Those who believe that passive smoking causes cancer think it increases the chance by about 30 per cent. Remember that, in the natural experiments that delivered this result, a passive smoker was defined as a non-smoker who lives with a smoker. So it does not follow that people who visit smoke-filled bars twice a week are 30 per cent more likely to get cancer. But, for simplicity, let's treat all passive smoking as being as bad as living with a smoker and say that it generally increases the chances of getting lung cancer by 30 per cent.

That sounds like a lot. But it sounds like less when you note that a non-smoker's chance of dying from lung cancer is only about 0.3 per cent. Being a passive smoker thus increases the chance to about 0.4 per cent: that is, it increases the chance by 0.1 percentage points. But the cost of this is not 0.1 per cent multiplied by your statistical cost of life, which, following the research, I will assume to be £4 million. This is because you will not lose your entire life. The lung cancer will not strike and kill you immediately. It will take some time to emerge. In fact, on average, lung cancer is diagnosed at 71 years of age. And even without treatment, life continues for a while afterwards. On average, you will lose about ten years of an expected 80, which is 12.5 per cent of your life. So the cost that passive smoking imposes on you by way of increasing your chance of lung cancer is £4,000,000 x 12.5 per cent x 0.1 per cent = £500.

Of course, passive smoking may cause not just lung cancer but other illnesses besides, such as heart disease. To avoid trawling through the disputed science again, and because it is of little importance to the following argument, let us be generous to the prohibitionists and double the health cost of passive smoking. This makes the total health cost of passive smoking about £1,000.

This is not an annual cost, but the lifetime health cost of being a passive smoker.[8] A one-off payment of £1,000 would compensate the average Briton for the increased chance of death they derive from decades of passive smoking. Or, to put it another way, a smoking wife could compensate her non-smoking husband by giving him £1,000 on their wedding day.

This means that the cleaning costs of living with a smoker almost certainly exceed the health costs. If you live with a smoker, and have a normal aversion to bad smells and discolouration, you will need to get your woollen jumpers, suits, curtains, furniture and carpets cleaned more frequently. And you will need to repaint the inside of your house more often.

Consider just the extra cost of keeping your suits clean. Suppose living with a smoker entailed two extra £15 suit dry-cleanings a year and that the marriage was expected to last 35 years. To compensate her husband for this expense, a smoking wife would have to give him £650 on their wedding day (assuming a 3 per cent discount rate). Add in the curtain cleaning, repainting, etc., and the cleaning cost of living with a smoker is greater than the £1,000 health cost.

'Passive smoking increases your chance of getting cancer by 33 per cent'. That is a headline that might agitate people, and even get them to support a law against smoking in enclosed public spaces. 'The lifetime health cost of passive smoking is £1,000 or about £1 a week'. That would not be so effective. So it

---

8   I omit the cost of medical treatment that people who contract cancer or other serious diseases undertake. This is because the sick person (or the NHS) would pay for these treatments only insofar as they cost less than they were worth in extra life expectancy (taking into account the quality of that extra life). So the cost of healthcare will be offset by a reduced cost of ill-health. Counting both the cost of medical care and the cost of ill-health would be double counting.

is unsurprising that advocates of the ban are inclined to make the former claim rather than the latter. But it is the latter claim that is relevant to decisions about whether or not to be a passive smoker, not the former.

The persistent announcements by health lobbyists and journalists about the percentage by which consumable X increases the chance of illness Y – doubling it, tripling it, quadrupling it or whatever – are irrelevant unless combined with the initial probability of getting that illness. Which they almost never are. Doubling the chance of something that has a minuscule chance of killing you leaves you with a tiny chance of dying from it. So it might easily be worth the cost. That's how it is with passive smoking. It has a small health cost even if it increases your chance of illness as much as the anti-passive smoking lobbyists say it does.

But this is all something of a red herring anyway. The size of the health cost of passive smoking, or even its existence, cannot be relevant to the ban on smoking in enclosed public spaces. The cleaning costs of passive smoking were well known before the health costs were allegedly discovered. And, as we have seen, the cleaning costs exceed the health costs of passive smoking. Yet they were never considered grounds for banning smoking in public places. Why not?

Voluntary passive smoking

It would be reckless to speculate on why legislators did not pass a law aimed at protecting people from the spillover cleaning costs of passive smoking. Perhaps it was mere apathy. But there is a good reason not to pass any such law, which, hopefully, explains their inaction. The reason can be seen by noting the absurdity of a popular alternative expression for passive smoking: namely, 'involuntary smoking'.[9]

Passive smoking is not involuntary. No one is obliged to marry a smoker or work in a smoky bar or do anything else that entails inhaling second-hand smoke. Yet many choose to do so, presumably because they think the benefits are worth the costs. They love their smoking spouses and consider living with them well worth the extra cleaning costs. Or they enjoy the company of their smoking friends and so are willing to spend time in unpleasantly smoky bars to be with them.

Not only is passive smoking voluntary but passive smokers can make active smokers feel the spillover costs. That is to say, they can do things that internalise the external costs of smoking and thereby ensure that the smoking occurs only if its total benefit exceeds its total cost (see Chapter 2). For example, they can complain to smokers, just as they complain to people who bring barking dogs into pubs or to neighbours who mow their lawns at 7 a.m. on Sundays. The host of a party can force smokers out into the cold street, or refuse to invite them in the first place. Or a passive-smoking husband might demand that his wife pays for his dry-cleaning.

Given the ease with which passive smoking can be avoided, and the ease with which active smokers can be made to feel the external costs, there is every reason to believe that roughly the right amount will occur without the help of politicians. A

---

9   Behold, for example, the title of this 2006 report on passive smoking by the Surgeon General of the US: *The Health Consequences of Involuntary Exposure to Tobacco Smoke: A Report of the Surgeon General*, US Department of Health and Human Services, Atlanta, 2006.

legislative intervention to prevent passive smoking can only result in a suboptimal amount of it.

In other words, applying a Pigouvian tax equal to the external cost of smoking would entail doubling up on the internalisation. A non-smoker who is unwilling to make smokers the gift of inhaling their second-hand smoke without complaint or any other retaliation will not change his behaviour on account of a tax on cigarettes. He will complain to a taxed smoker as much as to an untaxed one, since he does not receive the tax. This means that the smoker will be double-charged and will therefore be inclined to smoke less than the socially optimal amount. And if a Pigouvian tax is not justified by the external costs of smoking, a ban on smoking in enclosed public spaces certainly is not.

This logic apparently prevailed before the alleged discovery that passive smoking causes ill-health. Since legislators have become convinced of the health costs of passive smoking, however, they have abandoned it. This is peculiar. Ill-health, or the risk of it, is just another cost. Its discovery might tip the scales for some passive smokers, making them decide to avoid it or significantly increase the costs they impose on active smokers in their midst. But it does nothing to change the logic of the situation. Passive smoking is still voluntary and passive smokers still have ways of making active smokers feel the external costs.

Some may think that the *addition* of health costs to all the other known costs of passive smoking justifies the legislative intervention. Leaving the matter to those involved was acceptable while the cost of passive smoking was thought to be under £2,000. But the newly discovered health effects have pushed the spillover costs above some threshold for intervention.

No. The size of an avoidable spillover cost is irrelevant to the case for protective legislation. To see why, consider again 'kimchee breath', the unfortunate side effect of eating the Korean staple of spicy fermented cabbage. Those who eat kimchee impose a cost on those around them. Yet the government of Korea imposes no restrictions on kimchee eating. They do not need to because the spillover cost of kimchee breath redounds to kimchee eaters in the form of unpopularity – complaints, shunning and the like. So Korean kimchee eaters tend to practise extraordinary oral hygiene, brushing their teeth after every meal.

Suppose it was discovered that smelling kimchee was not only unpleasant but also slightly carcinogenic. Would this warrant legislation controlling the consumption of kimchee? No. The increased cost of being near kimchee eaters would increase the demand for kimchee-free restaurants, for kimchee-free sections on aeroplanes and so on. And it would increase the cost of being a kimchee eater by increasing the vehemence with which kimchee breath-smellers complained to their tormentors, shunned them and mocked them. In short, the amount of kimchee breath smelling would naturally decline in response to the increased cost of it. There would be no need for legislative intervention to protect kimchee breath-smellers.

The same goes for passive smoking. As the perceived cost of it increases – perhaps because health costs are added to cleaning costs – so people will go to greater lengths to avoid it. The demand for smoke-free places will increase and the cost of being a public smoker will increase. This will naturally decrease the quantity of passive smoking. There is no need for legislative intervention to protect passive smokers.

Ironically, this kind of market mechanism will most obviously work for precisely those passive smokers whose welfare the British ban was supposed to protect: namely, people working in bars and restaurants. If passive smoking is costly then the supply of people willing to work in smoky environments will be smaller than the supply willing to work in smoke-free environments. This will drive up the rates of pay offered to workers in smoky workplaces. Workers will have a choice between more pay and less safety or less pay and more safety. Some will prefer one trade-off, others the other. By banning one of these trade-offs, the law makes those who preferred it worse off and those who preferred the alternative no better off.

Not all passive smoking is voluntary. One group of passive smokers have little or no choice in the matter: namely, the children of smokers. They do most of their passive smoking at home and in the family car. And these unlucky children cannot choose different parents. There may be a case for legislation to protect children from their parents' smoking.

It is difficult to see how this could be achieved without simply banning the production, import or sale of cigarettes. Detecting smoking at home would require a level of surveillance that even the British government would probably find unacceptable. Perhaps the government will one day impose such a 'supply side' prohibition. As things stand, however, public policy probably has the effect of increasing the amount of involuntary passive smoking in Britain.

This is a result of the kind of substitution effects discussed in Chapter 2. A prohibition on smoking in enclosed public spaces will increase the amount of smoking in enclosed private spaces. Instead of going out to bars and restaurants, many smokers will now stay at home to eat and socialise. The rapid reduction in the number of people visiting pubs since the ban was introduced in

2007 strongly suggests that this is indeed happening.[10] The ban on smoking in enclosed public spaces has thus shifted the spillover costs of smoking from people who accepted them voluntarily on to children with no choice in the matter.

Bigotry-based policy

The prohibition on smoking in enclosed public spaces is a perfect example of evidence-based policy. Those promoting it expend great quantities of effort on trying to persuade us of the ill-effects of what they want banned. They seem to think success in this endeavour suffices to justify their policy. It does not. The policy is not in fact justified by the evidence or by the fact the evidence is supposed to establish: in this case, that passive smoking increases the chance of cancer. An activity that has spillover costs should not be prohibited when those costs are accepted voluntarily or are 'returnable': that is, when the person suffering them can impose retaliatory costs on the person causing them.

The spillover cleaning costs of smoking are both accepted voluntarily and returnable. Quite rightly, no government has imposed a ban on smoking in enclosed public spaces to protect passive smokers from these cleaning costs. The spillover health costs of passive smoking are also accepted voluntarily and returnable. Yet many governments have legislated to 'protect' passive smokers from these costs. Why? What is the relevant difference between cleaning costs and health costs?

Not the size of the harm. As we have seen, size doesn't matter.

---

10   In the years directly after the introduction of smoking bans in Ireland (2004), Scotland (2006), Wales (2007) and England (2007), the rate of net pub closures in each country accelerated markedly (CR Consulting, 2010).

And, in any case, the spillover cleaning costs of passive smoking are probably greater than the spillover health costs. The simple answer is that there is no relevant difference between these two kinds of spillover cost. But, whereas any Westerner, including any Western politician, would think it ludicrous to pass laws aimed at protecting people from dry-cleaning costs that they voluntarily accept, many Westerners, and especially Western politicians, think it quite reasonable to pass laws to protect people from health costs they voluntarily accept.

For example, few people find it odd that the law requires motorcyclists to wear helmets so as to reduce their chance of dying in an accident. Yet a proposal to legally oblige motorcyclists to wear cheap nylon overalls so as to reduce the cost of cleaning their clothes would strike almost everyone as absurd. You are generally free to decide for yourself what costs you are willing to bear for the sake of what benefits. But not when it comes to health. Health is a special kind of cost, which you may trade off only within constraints imposed by legislators.

No scientific evidence can show that trade-offs involving health should be subject to constraints that other trade-offs are not. Nor does any known ethical or economic theory show it. When legislators ban smoking in enclosed public spaces, or enact other laws aimed at making people lead healthy lives, they are not doing something required by evidence. Rather, they are imposing their own high regard for health on people who do not share it. That is not science. It is theocracy.

4 GLOBAL WARMING

In the 1970s, some scientists warned of an imminent ice age. *Time* magazine and many newspapers ran stories announcing the bad news. Climatic predictions deal in centuries or, at a pinch, periods of several decades. So it may be too early to judge the accuracy of these predictions. But, despite the recent spate of cold winters in Britain, it seems they were wrong.

This error has not discouraged predictions of climatic disaster. Since the late 1980s, many scientists have warned that carbon dioxide and other 'greenhouse gases' produced by industrial societies are causing temperatures to rise. This anthropogenic global warming (AGW) is alleged to be dangerous. The polar icecaps will melt, causing sea levels to rise and flood coastal cities. Fresh water supplies will collapse. Crops will fail. Starvation and mass migrations will cause social unrest, war and misery. It will be a disaster of biblical proportions.

To avert this disaster, which will allegedly develop over the coming century, many politicians and campaigners support measures aimed at reducing the emission of greenhouse gases. And many countries have adopted such measures. They tax electricity produced by burning fossil fuels, air travel, and cars with big gas-guzzling engines. They subsidise energy sources that do not burn fossil fuels, electric cars and home insulation. They impose 'cap and trade' systems, whereby firms that emit greenhouse gases must purchase tradable permits. And they cajole their populations, through schools and public media, to be sparing in their use of energy.

Despite these measures, the emission of greenhouse gases continues to rise, especially in large and newly industrialised countries such as China. Many claim that more stringent restrictions on emissions are required – yet higher carbon taxes, 'green' subsidies and legally binding national limits of the kind that were not agreed upon at the 2009 Climate Change Summit in Copenhagen. Lord Stern of Brentford, author of the 2006 *Review on the Economics of Climate Change* (commissioned by the UK government), has even claimed that eating meat could become 'socially unacceptable' because the practice maintains a large population of cows.[1] Cows are flatulent and the methane they emit is a greenhouse gas.

Such measures will be costly. By making energy more expensive, they will drive up the cost of food, manufactured goods, heating, travel and almost everything else. Some say the cost is too great, that it exceeds the benefits of reducing carbon emissions. Broadly speaking, there are two reasons for taking this view. The first is that AGW is not really occurring. This is the position of the so-called 'deniers'. The second is that, even if AGW is real, measures aimed at reducing carbon emissions will be an expensive waste of time. It would be wiser to incur costs to mitigate the harmful effects of global warming: for example, by building sea defences.

We will get to this second objection in the final section of this chapter. But the debate over the reality of AGW is my

---

1   Quoted in the *Guardian*, 26 October 2009.

principal concern because this is where the scientific nonsense occurs. Or, more precisely, this is where nonsense about science occurs. Barack Obama and the others who claim that 'the science is settled' display a remarkable ignorance either of the data, methods and predictive success of current climate science or of what the word 'settled' means.

But first, we must return to the logic of external costs and Pigouvian taxes.

AGW and Pigouvian taxes

Suppose that burning fossil fuels really is causing hazardous global warming. Unlike those of passive smoking, which is voluntary and hence calls for no policy response, the spillover costs of burning fossil fuels cannot be avoided by those who bear them. A coal-fired power station in China releases tonnes of carbon dioxide into the air, the temperatures rise, Arctic ice melts, sea levels rise, and the populations of Pacific atolls are driven from their homes. They have no choice in the matter. They did not decide to bear this cost for the sake of some benefit they receive from the Chinese power station.

This means that AGW looks like a proper area for policies aimed at internalising external costs. People who burn fossil fuels – by using coal-generated electricity, by driving a car that runs on petrol or whatever – do not bear the cost they impose on others via AGW. They will thus burn more fossil fuel than they should; they will burn it even when the total cost of doing so exceeds the total benefit (assuming that the external benefits do not exceed the external costs). Pigouvian carbon taxes are warranted. A tax on emitting carbon dioxide equal to its external cost would make sure that it happens only when its total benefit exceeds its total cost.

Of course, not all of the policies allegedly justified by AGW conform to this logic. For example, subsidising wind power will only increase the over-consumption of energy. A Pigouvian tax effectively eliminates a subsidy: in this case, the 'subsidy' enjoyed by fossil fuel burners who need pay nothing for the costs they impose on people through AGW. Subsidising an alternative to fossil fuels does not eliminate this subsidy; it merely creates a 'level playing field' for competing sources of energy. But it does so by giving all energy consumption a subsidy. If a proper Pigouvian tax were applied to fossil fuel consumption, no subsidy for alternatives would be warranted.

Nor do 'cap and trade' systems (usually applied only to large firms) mean that carbon will be emitted just when doing so delivers a net benefit. On these systems, the total amount of carbon emitted is capped by the number of permits issued and, as demand to emit carbon rises or falls, so the price of the tradable permits rises or falls. Only if the price of the permit is the same as the external cost of carbon emission will we get the right amount of it. Yet there is no reason why they should be the same. The price of permits is determined by the level of the cap and the demand to emit carbon. The external cost of carbon emissions is not.

But I do not mean to enter the debate about which policies aimed at restricting carbon emissions are best. All are intended to work by imposing costs on carbon emitters and the consumers of goods whose production emits carbon. So all raise the question of whether this cost is warranted by the benefit. For simplicity, we can think of all such measures as forms of Pigouvian tax and then ask whether the tax is roughly equal to the external cost of emitting carbon.

What, then, *is* the external cost of emitting carbon? The answer depends on climatic effects that are disputed, as discussed below. But it also depends on the preferences of those who experience the effects of AGW. In other words, it is not a question that can be settled by climate science alone.

Compare a builder from Oslo, a fisherman from the Pacific atoll of Tuvalu and a factory worker in Beijing. The Norwegian builder may benefit from AGW, since he works outdoors in a cold country. The Tuvalu fisherman will be seriously harmed by it, since he will be driven from his home and his livelihood. The factory worker in Beijing may be almost indifferent, since he already lives in an environment that is so polluted and unpleasant that making it hotter may cause little marginal pain. Of course, AGW may have effects that harm even our Norwegian builder. For example, he may find his taxes increased to fund the housing, education and other claims of refugees from Pacific atolls. But this does not change the fact that AGW will not impose its costs equally on everyone.

This means that, even if the effects of carbon emissions were known with certainty, it would be difficult to estimate the external cost. Not only would we need to know the preferences of people around the world but we would need to weigh them. Suppose our Tuvalu fisherman were willing to pay US$500 to eliminate the effects of AGW, the Beijing factory worker were willing to pay US$200 and our Oslo builder –US$500: that is, he would pay US$500 to bring them on. It does not follow that the net external cost of AGW for our little group is US$200. Consumption and, hence, the money that buys it have diminishing marginal value. US$500 is worth far more to the Tuvalu fisherman than it is to the much richer Norwegian builder. To calculate the aggregate effect on welfare – the true external cost – we would need to apply a 'welfare function' that assigns weights to the amounts of money people are willing to pay to avoid the effects of AGW (or to receive as compensation).

The same goes for the cost of Pigouvian taxes on carbon emissions. They do not fall equally on everyone. Our Tuvalu fisherman will suffer little from an increased cost of energy, since he consumes little to begin with. Our Norwegian builder will suffer more, since he consumes much energy to keep warm in his cold country and to do his job efficiently by using machinery. And our Beijing factory worker may suffer most. He works in an industry whose products will be made more expensive by the tax. This will reduce demand for them. He may suffer lower pay or even lose his job. And, again, all these costs would need to be weighted by a welfare function.

Discounting calamity

The difficulty of applying a welfare function and calculating the external cost of AGW is exacerbated by the fact that the alleged ill-effects of AGW are mainly several decades away. The costs will be borne almost entirely by people who have not yet been born. To estimate the external cost of AGW we must make assumptions about the preferences of these future people and about the levels and distribution of wealth among them.

Some such assumptions are reasonably safe. These future people will be like us in most respects. But their circumstances may differ from ours in ways that incline them to make different trade-offs from those we are inclined to make. They may live longer and enjoy more leisure time. And they may use their leisure in different ways – for example, spending much of it on indoor activities, such as today's online gaming. Because such developments are difficult to predict, it is also difficult to estimate the external cost of AGW.

Some economists argue that such potential changes in preferences mean we should increase our estimates of the external costs of environmental damage. For example, in a report on how to measure national wellbeing, commissioned by the French government, the economists Amartya Sen and Joseph Stiglitz claimed that:

> One could [try to] infer the definition of well-being from current observations of how people value environmental factors compared to economic ones, using contingent valuations or direct measures of the impact of environmental amenities on indexes of subjective well-being ...
>
> But can measures established today in a certain eco-environmental setting be used to predict what will be the valuations of future generations in eco-environmental settings that may have become very different? Some may argue that our descendants may become very sensitive to the relative scarcity of some environmental goods to which we pay little attention today because they are still relatively abundant, and that the precautionary principle should therefore require that we immediately place a high value on these items just because we think that our descendants may wish to do so. (Stiglitz et al., 2009: 75)

Perhaps future generations will indeed place a higher value on environmental goods than we do, even after adjusting for the fact that they will almost certainly be richer than us. But Sen and Stiglitz suggest that they will without providing any reason to believe it. In fact, there is a general reason to expect preferences to change in the opposite direction.

As Sen is usually keen to point out, preferences are generally adaptive (see, for example, Sen, 1999). That is to say, our preferences tend to adjust to our circumstances in ways that reduce the disappointment or other psychic pain they would otherwise cause. Parents often act as agents in this process, discouraging their children from aspiring to things they are unlikely to obtain.

The adaptive quality of preferences means that progressive adverse changes in our circumstances are likely to cause less pain than sudden ones, regardless of any difference in our ability to adapt our behaviour to them. For example, as the American population has become fatter over the last 50 years, more people have become unhappy about their figures. But this unhappiness is less than the unhappiness that would have been felt if, one morning in 1962, 100 million Americans had awoken to discover they had overnight put on 30 pounds of blubber.

The same goes for AGW. Given that preferences are adaptive, we ought to expect a deteriorating environment to cause future generations to value environmental goods less than we do today. People who live in what may be the dreadful environment of 2100 will not be as bothered by it as we would be. Without some special reason to believe otherwise, which Sen and Stiglitz do not supply, they seem to have got the matter precisely the wrong way around.

If preferences were perfectly adaptive, so that they instantly adjusted to the relative scarcity of goods, changes in our environment would be irrelevant to our welfare. Since nothing could improve or damage the environment, any investment in it would be pointless; the results would inevitably be worthless.

Of course, our preferences are not perfectly adaptive. Nor are they uniformly adaptive: we can adjust to some things more easily than others. But they are somewhat adaptive. And this warrants discounting, to some extent, the value we would today give to any future effects carbon taxes might have on the environment. By how much we should discount them, I will not pretend to know.

The fact that future generations will probably be richer than us also means that future benefits should be discounted when valuing current initiatives. As noted above, consumption has diminishing marginal value. If we did not discount the extra consumption of future, richer generations, we would be giving their welfare more weight than our own.[2]

Suppose long-run global per capita economic growth will continue at 2 per cent per annum, which it has recently exceeded. Then we should discount future costs and benefits by 2 per cent per annum. Add a modest 'preference adaptation discount' of only 1 per cent, and we have a discount rate of 3 per cent. Yet in his 2006 review of climate change, Sir Nicholas Stern applied a discount rate of only 1.5 per cent (Stern, 2006).

By using a peculiarly low discount rate, Lord Stern skewed his analysis in favour of incurring costs today for the sake of future benefits. And, as you might then expect, his report concluded that

---

2   A common justification for discounting future benefits is the simple fact that we do not care about future people, including our future selves, as much as we care about present people. When making decisions that trade off current and future consumption, people discount future consumption more than is warranted by adjustments for factors such as increasing expected incomes. But this fact about private spending decisions ought to be irrelevant to public policy. We care less about people in far-off places than we care about our families and neighbours. That may explain our private behaviour. But it does not justify public policies that deliver a net benefit only if we discount foreigners' welfare relative to our own. In other words, it does not license predatory policies. Similarly, we do not care about people at far-off times. But so what? Just as far-off foreigners' welfare is not made unimportant by the fact that we do not care much about them, nor is the welfare of future people made unimportant by our relative indifference to them.

expensive measures to cut carbon emissions today are warranted by their future environmental benefits.[3]

Several commentators have claimed that this is a fatal flaw in his report.[4] Perhaps it is. But I will not pursue this issue, for the argumentative tactic of those who favour expensive measures to cut carbon emissions is to swamp all such quibbling about discount rates with projections of doom if we do not soon follow their policy. Or, to put it the other way around, they project future benefits for their policy so great that no realistic discount rate can be large enough to undermine the case for it. For example, Lord Stern has responded to criticism of his 2006 review by saying: 'We underestimated the risks ... we underestimated the damage associated with temperature increases ... and we underestimated the probabilities of temperature increases.'[5]

Perhaps the policies recommended to reduce carbon emissions really will save us from a climatic catastrophe; we will turn to this question in the next section. But it is worth noting the strong temptation of policy campaigners to be doom merchants.

All policies create costs and benefits, winners and losers. Deciding whether a policy makes the best trade-off can be a difficult business, subject to arcane considerations, such as the proper discount rate to apply, and to all manner of uncertainties, such

---

3   Even my 3 per cent is low. Some economists argue that the proper discount rate is the one currently applied to equity investments: that is, the opportunity cost of capital (which these days is about 6 per cent to 20 per cent or higher, depending on the risk of the investment). After all, future generations will want us to invest our current resources in whatever way delivers the best return on them. Applying a lower discount rate to the benefits or costs incurred to cut carbon emissions skews investment in this direction – which harms future generations by diverting resources away from better investments.

4   See, for example, Nordhaus (2007) and Weizman (2007).

5   Quoted in the *Financial Times*, 16 April 2008.

as the preferences of unknown people in far-off places. For the earnest campaigner, such matters can prove an unwanted impediment to 'moving forward'. If only all this debate could be brushed aside. If only everyone could see that the policy is a 'no brainer'.

Hence the appeal of impending catastrophe. Preferences may vary but everyone wants to live. Confronted with Armageddon, no one will quibble about welfare functions and discount rates. This may explain why policy campaigners and their expert supporters are so quick to predict catastrophe.

Any British citizen over the age of 40 might consider himself lucky to be alive today. He has survived an AIDS epidemic, which we were told in the late 1980s would have killed many millions of Britons by the year 2000 (but had in fact killed only 20,000 by 2010).[6] He has survived the variant Creutzfeldt-Jakob Disease (vCJD) epidemic, caused by its bovine equivalent, bovine spongiform encephalopathy (BSE), which in 1997 was going to kill hundreds of thousands of us (but has actually killed 170 over 17 years). He survived SARS in 2003, bird flu in 2007, swine flu in 2009 and at this very moment may be surviving the epidemics of drinking- and obesity-related diseases that are causing a 'public health crisis'. No generation of persistently doomed people has lived longer. Indeed, no generation has lived longer, doomed or not.

---

6 The government's 1986 advertising campaign designed to save us from AIDS claimed that 'AIDS does not discriminate'. This was well known to be false even in 1986. Rates of AIDS were much higher in homosexuals and in intravenous drug users than in the rest of the population, an unsurprising fact given the transmission mechanism for HIV. I will not speculate on why the government intentionally misled people about their relative chances of contracting AIDS.

Risk and uncertainty

Is catastrophic AGW really likely to occur if we do not reduce carbon emissions? That is the central question for policymakers being encouraged to take expensive measures to avert it. They cannot become experts on the topic. The prime minister and other politicians who must decide on the proper policy cannot become climate scientists. Rather, they must form an opinion about the reliability of the prediction of catastrophic AGW.

No empirical science or its predictions can be completely beyond doubt. But scientific theories can achieve high degrees of certainty, so that their predictions can be relied upon when forming policy. Physics provides the paradigm example. The ultimate constituents of nature and the fundamental laws may still be matters of active research but the physics that some public policy depends on – for example, the physics that under-pins building regulations – is so reliable that doubt about it could never be a serious issue in policy debate. If someone disapproves of a policy of building regulations, it will not be because he doubts the physics.

Climate science is not as certain as physics. But is it sufficiently certain to provide a proper basis for public policy?

First, a common confusion between risk and uncertainty must be avoided. Risk concerns the probability of adverse events. Certainty concerns our knowledge of those probabilities. Suppose you are playing roulette and considering betting on black. If the table is fair – that is, if it is not adjusted in a way that skews the apparent probabilities given by the number of red, black and 'house' slots – then your chance of losing your bet is 0.52. That is the risk.

But you cannot be certain that this is the risk, because you cannot be certain that the table is fair. If you are rational, your certainty will vary with evidence about the casino. Is it well maintained, owned by a company with a valuable brand, lacking a history of scandal, etc.? You know that, on the theory that this is a fair table, your risk of losing is 0.52. Your problem is to assess the certainty of this theory.[7]

Alas, discussions of climate policy often obscure this distinction, with the result that they sometimes end up taking the uncertainty of climate science as a positive reason for bearing costs to avoid climatic risks. Consider this paragraph from the introduction of Sir Nicholas Stern's 2006 review:

> We use a consistent approach towards uncertainty. The science of climate change is reliable, and the direction is clear. But we do not know precisely when and where particular impacts will occur. Uncertainty about impacts strengthens the argument for mitigation: this Review is about the economics of the management of very large risks. (Stern, 2006: 1)

By 'uncertainty' in the first of the quoted sentences, Stern seems to be referring to the probabilistic nature of the climate theories he relies upon. They do not say what will happen where and when. Instead, they assign probabilities to various outcomes. In other words, they describe risks. But it is misleading to call these risks 'uncertainty', because you are all too likely to end up drawing Stern's absurd conclusion that 'uncertainty about the impacts strengthens the argument for mitigation'.

---

7   The reports accepted by of the Intergovernmental Panel on Climate Change (IPCC) since 2001 have distinguished between risk, which they call the likelihood of an event, and certainty, which they call the confidence that a statement is true. They attribute confidence to statements in five intervals ranging from 'very low' to 'very high'.

Consider alien abduction insurance (which is, in fact, available). Suppose a £10 annual premium buys a policy that pays out £10 million should you be abducted. This is a good deal if your annual chance of being abducted is greater than one in a million. As this risk increases, so the insurance becomes a better deal at this price. But that is quite different from saying that, as the certainty that you will be abducted declines – in other words, as the uncertainty increases – so the insurance becomes a better deal. On the contrary, as the certainty or credibility of the theory that aliens visit Earth and abduct people declines, so the rational man will become *less* willing to buy the insurance policy, no matter what the implausible theory says about the risk of alien abduction.[8]

The Stern review and other 'authoritative' cost–benefit analyses assign probabilities to various climatic outcomes. But these are taken directly from climate models, which are thereby treated as being beyond reasonable doubt. By saying that they take 'a consistent approach to uncertainty' and by assigning probabilities to different outcomes, such reports might give the casual reader the impression that their recommendations survive a healthy degree of scepticism about current climate science. Such readers would be misled.

---

8   Ross Garnaut provides an explicit discussion of the difference between risk and uncertainty in Chapter 1.2 of his 2008 review of the economics of climate change for the Australian government (Garnaut, 2008). Alas, he becomes so confused that he claims that risk and uncertainty lie at either end of a single spectrum. A spectrum of what? The idea suggests that as risk declines, uncertainty increases. This is nonsense. Something can be both very risky and very uncertain, and vice versa.

The science is not settled

The forecasts for AGW relied upon by the Intergovernmental Panel on Climate Change (IPCC) and other authorities are derived from modern climate science and, especially, from general circulation models (GCMs). How credible are these models and the climate science behind them? Or, more precisely, how much credence should we give their predictions of a calamitous man-made increase in the global climate in several decades' time?

The obvious problem is that modern climate science and GCMs are relatively new. We have not had time to see whether their predictions for the global climate 50 years hence are generally accurate. Indeed, even in 50 years we will have only one data point, which is hardly sufficient to confirm the predictive reliability of a model.

This difficulty is exacerbated by the fact that we do not know what the climate would be in 50 years' time if the climate models that predict AGW were false. In other words, we do not know what the climate would be if the null hypothesis were correct. No one denies that the climate changes even without any human influence. But, without depending on the very models we seek to test, we cannot predict the future climate without the effects of greenhouse gases. This means that we do not know which future climatic observations would confirm the AGW hypothesis and which would disconfirm it.

'Retrodiction' or 'hindcasting' – that is, plugging in data from a past date (such as 1800) and then predicting the climate at a subsequent past date (such as 1850) – cannot help. Retrodictive success is unimpressive when a model has many parameters (input variables), as GCMs do. Modern computing power means that it is a simple task to make a multi-variable model fit even large quantities of observed data. As the mathematician and computer scientist John von Neumann put it, 'with four parameters I can fit an elephant, and with five I can make him wiggle his trunk'.[9]

Nor can the reliability of short-term predictions be extrapolated to a presumed reliability of long-term predictions. This is a generally unsound form of reasoning. For example, I have so far been very good at predicting whether or not I will be alive tomorrow. But no one should take this as evidence that I am a good judge of whether I will be alive in 40 years' time.

In the case of AGW and climate science, however, no such general objection is required. Climate models are unreliable when making short-term predictions. Those who predict AGW claim that climate science is more reliable in its long-term predictions than in its short-term predictions. In other words, extrapolation from short-term predictive success cannot be the foundation of confidence in the predictions of AGW.

What, then, is the foundation? How do those who advise policymakers justify the high levels of confidence they recommend for the untested reliability of climate models? Three justifications are commonly offered.

Climate science is simply physics

Most models of the climate are based on known laws of physics.[10] For example, laws about how gases propagate heat play a role

9   Attributed to von Neumann by Enrico Fermi, as quoted by Freeman Dyson (2004).
10   Some climate models are purely statistical. That is, they work by finding patterns in past climate data and then assuming these will persist in the future, without any attempt to identify their underlying causes.

in the models that predict rising temperatures on the basis of increased levels of carbon dioxide in the atmosphere. This tempts some AGW campaigners and even some scientists to conclude that the predictions of climate models are as dependable as those of physics. For example, according to Professor Stephan Lewandowsky and Professor Michael Ashley,

> We can calculate the effect, and predict what is going to happen to the earth's climate during our lifetimes, all based on fundamental physics that is as certain as gravity ...
>
> The consensus opinion of the world's climate scientists is that climate change is occurring due to human CO_2 emissions. The changes are rapid and significant, and the implications for our civilization may be dire. The chance of these statements being wrong is vanishingly small.[11]

The idea that climate models inherit the certainty of the physical laws that they include and, hence, that their predictions are as dependable as the prediction that dropped objects will fall (a comparison made explicitly by Lewandowsky and Ashley) is preposterous.

This reasoning is an almost perfect example of the fallacy of composition. An object made up of many small parts need not also be small. Similarly, a theory that is based on many statements, each of which is 99.9 per cent certain, need not itself be 99.9 per cent certain. Wholes do not necessarily inherit the qualities of their parts, nor vice versa. An author who believes with 99 per cent confidence each individual statement in his book does

---

11 'The false, the confused and the mendacious: how the media gets it wrong on climate change', *The Conversation*, 24 June 2011. Stephan Lewandowsky is Australian Professorial Fellow at the Cognitive Science Laboratories, University of Western Australia. Michael Ashley is Professor of Astrophysics at the University of New South Wales.

not contradict himself when he writes in the preface that the book almost certainly contains errors.

One can doubt climate models without doubting the physics they are built on. This is made obvious by the fact that physicists do not worry about the predictive inaccuracy of climate models – neither the actual inaccuracy of their short-term predictions nor the potential inaccuracy of their long-term predictions. Physicists do not consider the predictions of climate models to constitute a test of current physical theory. If climatic predictions are wrong, no one will conclude that our current view of the laws of physics is wrong. We will conclude that the laws employed by climate models did not give a complete picture of the causes of climatic events.

Even if everything in climate models comes from uncontroversial parts of physics and chemistry, it does not follow that these parts of physics and chemistry are adequate to explain and predict climatic events and trends. Imagine I offered a theory aimed at predicting how long it will take paper darts to fall to the floor after being thrown. My theory makes this time a function of gravity alone. It would thereby contain nothing but an uncontroversial part of physics. But it would do a bad job of predicting flight times, because much more than gravity is at work in determining how long paper darts stay aloft.

How, then, should we decide whether the physical laws invoked in climate models really are sufficient to predict climatic events or trends 50 years hence? The obvious answer is that we must determine whether these models are missing such elements by testing them, by seeing how accurately they predict future climatic events. But, as already noted, we cannot. It is precisely because the long-term predictive accuracy of these models cannot now be tested that their inclusion of physical laws was appealed to. Yet we now see that this appeal is of little value unless we can test the resulting climatic theories. For, unless we can, we will not know if the physics drawn upon is sufficient to the task of predicting the climate.

Some may now think my earlier dismissal of retrodiction was too quick. If a climate model that contains nothing but uncontroversial laws of physics can retrodict the climate – if plugging in the 1800 data causes it to spit out accurate 1850 data, and similarly for other such intervals – does this not suggest that the climate model can be relied upon? If a climate model contains only laws of physics, concerns about 'data fitting' are misguided; you cannot adjust the laws of physics to fit the data.

Alas, climate models do not contain only statements of the laws of physics: $F=ma$, $e=mc^2$, $g=(m+m)/d^2$, and so on. It would be more accurate to say that they contain (putative) laws relating elements of the climate and their various causes that are consistent with the laws of physics. For example, they specify relationships between greenhouse gas concentrations and heat propagation and between solar activity and sea temperatures. But the strength of these relationships cannot be derived from known physical laws. The models thus go beyond physics. Without contradicting any known physical law, different models can assign different strengths to their various relationships and, indeed, even include different sets of relationships. This means that the problem of data fitting, which makes retrodictive success unimpressive for multi-parameter computer models, does apply to climate models after all.

Indeed, the great variety of climate models that have been developed in recent years testifies to the fact that they are not entailed by known physical laws. If known physical laws entailed climate models, there would be only one climate model, not dozens.

There are many different models and they all predict AGW

When the long-term predictive reliability of climate models cannot be tested, their great variety ought to reduce our confidence in them. It suggests that they are only loosely based on the known laws of physics. Yet in the 'Summary for Policy Makers' of the 2007 IPCC report, the variety of climate models was claimed to be a source of increased confidence in the prediction of AGW: 'A major advance of this assessment of climate change projections compared with the TAR [Third Assessment Report] is the large number of simulations available from a broader range of models' (IPCC, 2007: 12).

To see the absurdity of this idea, consider the prediction that when you die, you will be judged by Jesus and sent to Heaven if you are deemed good. Until Martin Luther's famous protest, there were only a handful of theories (religions) suggesting this. After it, the number of theories suggesting it increased dramatically. In 1300 we had only Roman Catholicism and Orthodox Christianity. There are now hundreds of Christian models that make this prediction. If we were to follow the thinking of the IPCC, we would conclude that this increased diversity of Christianity also increased the confidence we ought to have in the prediction of an afterlife.

Or imagine yourself a policymaker. A scientist comes to you predicting doom on the basis of a computer model he has built. 'How reliable are the predictions of this model?' you ask. He admits that its short-term predictions are unreliable and that its long-term predictions have not been tested. You tell him to go away. The next week he returns with ten more untested models that also predict doom. According to the IPCC, this is 'a major advance' and you ought to abandon your previous scepticism. Anyone else would take such easy creation of new models, unaccompanied by any new predictive success, as a ground for increased scepticism.

It's the scientific consensus

Anyone with even a passing interest in AGW will have heard that most scientists believe it really is happening. Open letters stating belief in AGW, signed by hundreds of scientists, have been published by newspapers. Others have been published, also signed by many scientists, expressing doubts about AGW. But let us agree that among scientists, the balance of opinion is strongly on the side of the AGW thesis. What is the relevance of this fact?

Note, first, that this consensus should be of no relevance to those who work in climate science. A climate scientist cannot properly justify his confidence in the accuracy of a climate model by saying that others believe it. The confidence of non-expert outsiders may properly be based on the confidence of experts (see Chapter 6). But the confidence of the experts themselves must be based on evidence.

Yet this is the issue at stake. The climate models that predict AGW have not been tested and they are not mere entailments of well-known physics and chemistry. Why, then, do scientists have such high levels of confidence in them? In other words, if a scientific consensus really does exist, this is what needs to be explained. It cannot explain itself, nor justify itself.

According to the 2007 IPCC report's 'Summary for Policymakers', confidence in the elements and output of these models is often the result of 'expert judgement' (IPCC, 2007: 2, note 5). 'Expert judgement' refers to the opinions of people deemed experts. It ought to be irrelevant to scientists. Science progresses by ignoring mere opinion, expert or otherwise. If a theory has not been tested and confirmed, and is not entailed by something confirmed, then the opinions of scientists about its likely truth are of no particular value. When scientists express such opinions, they are not doing science. A statement or prediction is scientific, in the sense of warranting our credence, because of the way it is arrived at, not because a scientist says it (see also Chapter 6).

We do not have confidence in the predictions of physics because physicists say we should. Rather, our confidence is founded on the extraordinary success of physics. Physical theory does not merely allow us to anticipate the existence and location of previously unobserved planets or the speed at which little trolleys will travel across school science laboratories; it allows us to build televisions, spaceships, microwave ovens and so on. Physicists inherit their credibility from physics, not vice versa. That is why their special credibility is restricted to physics.

Those who build climate models are scientists. But their branch of science has no success with which to impress us, neither in its predictions nor in its applications. In the absence of such success, their assertions of confidence should carry little weight. Especially when such assertions are predictable even in the absence of proper grounds for confidence.

To understand the inclination of those working on immature branches of science to overstate the warranted level of confidence, consider the recent history of financial-risk modelling as applied to banking.

A bank's credit rating depends on the chance that it will become insolvent. This, in turn, depends on the risks the bank is taking and the quantity of capital it holds. The capital is a buffer against the losses that may result from the risks taken. The greater the ratio of the capital to the risks, the lower the likelihood that the bank will default on its obligations and the higher its credit rating.

It is a relatively simple matter to know how much capital a bank holds. But how likely are losses in excess of this amount: that is, in excess of the buffer that protects creditors? This probability is what a bank's credit rating properly depends on. Alas, it is difficult to know. A bank will have many thousands of 'risk exposures': loans to firms or consumers who may not repay them, assets denominated in foreign currencies that may devalue against the bank's domestic currency, investments in shares and bonds that may lose value and so on. And these risks will be correlated to greater or lesser extents, so that if the bank suffers one loss it is more or less likely to also suffer others. Knowing the probability of any given loss on such complex portfolios of risks is an extraordinary intellectual challenge.

Yet, by the early 21st century, 'risk modellers', applying theoretical advances in statistical finance, claimed they had cracked it. And regulators of the banking industry also believed they had, compelling banks to hold capital buffers calculated by these new risk models.

This was an apparently strange conviction. These models had no history of predictive success. Indeed, it was impossible for their estimates of 'tail risk' – that is, losses resulting from very unlikely events – to be tested, since very unlikely events do not happen often enough to test the models' estimates. Yet these tail risks are precisely the estimates that banks' capital requirements were based on. Nor were these risk models mere entailments of other theories that had already been confirmed.

Under such circumstances, the confidence placed in these models may surprise readers. But it should not. Start with the risk modellers themselves. They were natural enthusiasts for the models they had built, keen to believe that they had made valuable intellectual progress. They were hardly likely to err on the side of caution when assessing the credibility of their models. More importantly, they were paid to apply their models at banks, often many millions of dollars. In this enterprise, again, you can hardly expect them to have been cautious in the levels of confidence they expressed.

Now consider the authorities who encouraged banks to adopt these models. They had taken it upon themselves to specify the amount of capital that banks must hold to make themselves safe: that is, to have a probability of defaulting in the next year below some specified level, such as 0.05 per cent. If this quantity could not really be known with any certainty, the regulators would have been unable to perform the task they had taken for themselves. So they too were predisposed to overestimate the credence that should be given to these new risk models.

The same temptations are present with climate science. The scientists themselves are natural enthusiasts for their models and also benefit, by way of publicity and research grants, if others are also overconfident – especially if their science seems not only credible but important, which it does if it predicts avoidable disaster. And, just as modern politicians take it upon themselves to assure the safety of the financial system, so they like to assure the physical welfare of their populations. An unpredictable and uncontrollable climate is an affront to the ambitions of such politicians. So they too are keen to believe in the reliability of climate science.[12]

Beyond such motivated overconfidence, an ambiguity may explain some of the strong statements made by scientists and the authorities who act on their theories. Return for a moment to the case of risk modelling. Suppose it is 2003 and you had been employed to build a model that will tell a bank's executives how much capital is needed to cover the risks being taken. One day you bump into the bank's chief financial officer by the water cooler and he asks you: 'Do you really believe in this risk model you are building?'

Suppose that the model you are building is state of the art and takes account of all the available data. No better estimate of a bank's capital requirement can be made. You may well answer, in good conscience, that yes, you believe in the model.

Yet this is consistent with the proper level of certainty in the predictions of the model being low. The best that is now possible might not be very good. A rational person might accept the predictions of this model ahead of any others; he may have more confidence in this model than in any other. But he may still

---

12 Some have argued that many politicians accept the prediction of catastrophic AGW because measures aimed at preventing it are already congenial to them. That humans should consume less and that governments should control the use of resources were popular ideas before their adherents were so easily convinced by predictions of AGW. I do not pursue this line mainly because it is far stronger than anything needed to explain why the AGW prediction is likely to enjoy more certainty – or, at least, stronger statements of certainty – than is warranted by the evidence for it.

have a low level of confidence. And it is this low level of proper confidence that is relevant for deciding how to act in response to the model's predictions. The fact that more reliable predictions cannot be obtained from another source is irrelevant.

Current climate modelling may represent mankind's best efforts to understand and predict the climate, so that no alternative predictions are more reliable. This may warrant some kind of endorsement. It may incline some to say that they believe in these models. But such endorsement should not be taken to show that the models and their predictions warrant a high level of certainty.

Uncertainty and climate policy

The predictions of theories that have not been tested, and are not entailed by well-known facts, do not warrant high levels of certainty. Those who insist on this are not 'anti-science', as they are often claimed to be. On the contrary, it is those who are willing to be convinced in the absence of predictive success who display an unscientific cast of mind. The predictions of AGW may well be true but the certainty we should have in them falls well short of the certainty properly enjoyed by the predictions of physics. Those scientists who say otherwise – who claim that the predictions of climate science warrant as much confidence as predictions based on gravity, or that the AGW thesis is 'settled' – do not promote the public understanding of science.

Given this uncertainty, how should policymakers proceed? The first step to answering this question is to note that we are all policymakers. You cannot impose policies on your neighbours, as the politicians of your own country can, but you can decide your own climate policy. For example, you can decide to emit less carbon dioxide or make your house flood-resistant or move to higher ground or migrate to Norway. What will you do?

Reducing your carbon emissions by reducing your consumption of fossil fuels looks like a foolish personal policy. This is not only because of the doubt about the AGW thesis. The obvious problem is that your carbon emissions are a tiny proportion of the global total. Unless a large portion of the world's population decreases its consumption, your efforts will do nothing to reduce the chance of AGW. Worse, your reduced fossil fuel consumption will increase others' consumption. By reducing aggregate demand for fossil fuel, you will slightly lower its price, which will slightly increase the amount consumed by others. You will be making a tiny gift to people who do not worry about AGW as much as you do.

It may seem that, unlike individual policymakers, political policymakers do not face this problem. Politicians can make everyone, and not only themselves, consume less fossil fuel by imposing taxes that increase its price. But they cannot. Politicians can impose taxes only on their own populations, not the populations of other countries. If the British government imposes taxes that reduce fossil fuel consumption in Britain, the global price of fossil fuel will fall and people in other countries will consume more. The cost incurred by the British population will do nothing to reduce the chance of AGW. This is why those who want taxes and regulations to limit carbon emissions seek not only domestic policies, such as those already adopted in Britain, but international agreements which commit all governments to such policies.

But is this a sensible ambition to pursue? Nothing in climate science can tell us how likely it is that such international agreements will be made or that countries will not afterwards break ranks or that the black market in fossil fuel will not expand. Given the history of failure to agree such international policies, most recently in Copenhagen in 2009, a high degree of confidence seems unwarranted. Add to this the uncertainty about the AGW thesis, and pursuing the policy of cutting carbon emissions looks misguided.

These concerns do not apply to various other climate policies that you, as an individual, might adopt. Depending on where you live, you are at risk of flooding even if the climate is not warming. And the climate might warm even if the AGW hypothesis is false. So the various adaptations that can be made to lessen climatic risks might be warranted even if you are an AGW denier. Perhaps you really should move to higher ground or add hurricane blinds to your home or sell your farm in Texas and buy land in Newfoundland. And, unlike when cutting your carbon emissions, you can benefit from these adaptations even if others do not join in. Indeed, others' failure to join you will only increase your benefits. For example, if you are the first Texan farmer to relocate to Newfoundland you will sell your Texas farm while it is still worth something and buy the Newfoundland farm while it is still cheap.

But should you actually do such things? If AGW is uncertain, and if the future climate even without AGW is uncertain, how can you decide which adaptive policies are wise? The short answer is that you need only respond to market prices. Suppose you live in a location prone to flooding. If the AGW hypothesis proves correct or if flooding becomes more likely for other reasons, the cost of insuring your home against flood damage will increase. The increasing cost of such insurance provides a 'price signal' to shift out of the area. Similarly, farmers operating in areas with worsening climatic conditions (for whatever reason) will find their cost of capital increasing along with the climate-induced threat to their earnings. This will provide a price signal to move farming out of such areas and into those with better climatic prospects.

These adaptations to climate change will occur without any direction from governments. Insurers and investors have a private interest in adjusting the prices they charge to changing risks, and businesses and households have private interests in responding to those changing prices. No government policy is called for.

However, such adaptation requires a change in the policies of most governments – or, more accurately, it requires some policies to be eliminated. Governments now actively discourage adaptation to climatic change by subsidising climatic risk-taking. For example, the US federal government spent billions of dollars repairing damage done by the massive flooding that devastated much of New Orleans in 2006. This transferred the cost from people living in an area prone to flooding to people who do not. It therefore dampened the climatic risk price signal and the incentive to adapt to the climate. Such subsidies are not unique to the USA. Most governments use general tax revenues to compensate those who suffer the consequences of living in risky places.

Similarly, agricultural policies encourage people to farm where they should not. This is sometimes achieved by subsidising water for irrigation – a policy popular in dry places around the world. But it is the widespread use of agricultural trade barriers that causes the largest misallocation of farmland globally. Of course, preventing agricultural production from adapting properly to the global climate is not what motivates politicians to subsidise their own farmers and impose tariffs on imports from more efficient foreign producers. Nevertheless, that is what their policies achieve. Through these policies they have already brought about what they fear will be caused by climate change: namely, a world in which agricultural production is more costly than it could be because it does not fit the climate.

Some sensible climatic adaptations, such as sea defences, may be public goods that will therefore be undersupplied by the private sector. Here a policy may be required. But, unlike reductions in carbon emissions, these can be delivered by national governments. The benefits of a sea defence for London do not depend on other governments also building sea defences. There is no need for international agreements, nor any threat from other countries breaking ranks. Nor does their value depend on the AGW thesis; any source of rising tides will do, anthropogenic or not.

I will not spell out this approach to climate policy. Others have already done so (for example, Lawson, 2008) and, more importantly, it is surplus to the requirements of this chapter. My object has not been to argue for any particular climate policy but only to debunk the common idea that policies aimed at cutting carbon emissions are no more than obvious implications of solid science, and that anyone opposed to them is 'unscientific', a 'denier' or in some other way beyond the intellectual pale.

5 HAPPINESS ENGINEERING

Jigme Dorji Wangchuck, the former King of Bhutan, declared in 1972 that 'gross national happiness is more important than gross national product'.[1] The Centre for Bhutan Studies dutifully constructed a survey-based measure of GNH, whose increase is now the goal of Bhutan's five-year plans.

Wangchuckism did not initially catch on outside the 'happy kingdom'. But since the turn of the century, the idea has been gaining ground with Western politicians. They have not been inspired by the debatable success of the political pursuit of happiness in Bhutan; miserable people seeking a better life in another country still seem to prefer the USA, Europe and Australia to Bhutan. Rather, Western politicians have been drawn to Wangchuckism by alleged advances in the scientific study of happiness.

For example, in July 2006, David Cameron, then the leader of the opposition, gave his shadow cabinet their summer reading list. It included the recently published *Happiness: Lessons from a New Science* by Lord Richard Layard of Highgate, a professor of economics at the London School of Economics. In this book Layard explains the methods and findings of the new science of

---

1   See 'The background of gross national happiness', GNH Centre Bhutan, http://www.gnhbhutan.org/about/The_background_of_Gross_National_Happiness.aspx.

happiness and argues that public policy could be greatly improved by heeding them (Layard, 2005).

Shortly after becoming prime minister, David Cameron ordered the Office for National Statistics to develop a measure of the wellbeing of the British population. Its first report was published in July 2012. On average, the people of Britain are 7.3 happy, the maximum possible being 10 and the minimum 0 (ONS, 2012).

Similar initiatives have occurred elsewhere. In 2008, President Sarkozy commissioned the economists Joseph Stiglitz and Amartya Sen to construct a measure of French happiness (Stiglitz et al., 2009). The United Nations, World Bank, European Commission and Organisation for Economic Co-operation and Development also now measure not only wealth but wellbeing.

The information collected by the Office for National Statistics and these other organisations will do more than provide an after-the-fact measure of the success of public policy. It will add to the data available to scientists, such as Daniel Kahneman[2] and Richard Layard, who seek to discover the causes of happiness and misery. With such knowledge, some of which has already been acquired, public policy can be changed in ways that will increase our happiness. According to Layard, for example, the government should discourage work with high taxes (because leisure makes people happier than work does); it should restrict people's freedom of movement (because mobility reduces community spirit and thereby makes people unhappy); it should ban advertising to children (because advertising escalates their wants and

2   Daniel Kahneman is Nobel laureate in economics and emeritus professor of psychology at Princeton University. He is the leading figure in the academic study of happiness.

thus makes them unhappy); and it should impose a curriculum on schools requiring them to teach Layard's favoured list of 'the principles of morality not as interesting topics for discussion but as established truths to hold on to, essential for a meaningful life' (Layard, 2005: 233–4).

And these measures are just for starters. Layard recommends a thorough-going policy programme aimed at increasing gross national happiness. The alleged 'new science' of happiness will be to this social engineering what physics is to mechanical engineering.

Even if gross national happiness were a proper goal of government policy – which, as I show below, it is not – such social engineering would be an alarming prospect. For the 'science of happiness' is not even a pale imitation of proper sciences, such as physics. It is a parody of proper science. Basing public policy on modern happiness research is an outrageous idea, like building bridges on the basis of Aristotelian physics or developing medical treatments based on homeopathy.

The simplest way to show this is to examine the measure of happiness used to develop and test hypotheses about the causes of happiness, not only by happiness academics, such as Layard, but now also by the Office for National Statistics.

Measuring happiness

The Office for National Statistics (ONS) measures our happiness by asking four questions as part of the Integrated Household Survey:

- Overall, how satisfied are you with your life nowadays?

- Overall, how happy did you feel yesterday?
- Overall, how anxious did you feel yesterday?
- Overall, to what extent do you feel the things you do in your life are worthwhile?

Respondents are asked to give an answer from 0 to 10, with 0 being the minimum, meaning 'not at all', and 10 the maximum, meaning 'completely'.

Do not let the simplicity of these questions make you doubt the effort that went into choosing them. When deciding how to measure subjective wellbeing, the ONS consulted leading happiness experts. Indeed, its methodology paper on the topic, *Measuring Subjective Wellbeing for Public Policy* (Dolan et al., 2011), was written by Richard Layard, Paul Dolan, another happiness economist from the London School of Economics, and Robert Metcalfe, a behavioural economist at Oxford University.

Dolan, Layard and Metcalfe begin by setting out the standards that must be met by a measure of subjective wellbeing that is 'useful' for appraising and designing policy. It must be 'theoretically *rigorous*, policy *relevant* and empirically *robust*': a new three-Rs for policy wonks. But what do these requirements amount to? Dolan et al. tell us:

> By theoretically rigorous, we mean that the account of wellbeing is grounded in an accepted philosophical theory. By policy relevant, we mean that the account of wellbeing must be politically and socially acceptable, and also well understood in policy circles. By empirically rigorous, we mean that the account of wellbeing can be measured in a quantitative way that suggests that it is reliable and valid as an account of wellbeing. (Ibid.: 4)

The empirically robust condition is the important one, and is discussed in the next section. But it is worth pausing for a moment on the first two requirements.

The idea that an account of subjective wellbeing is theoretically rigorous because it is 'grounded in an accepted philosophical theory' is difficult to take seriously. Some philosophical theory is rigorous; some is incoherent nonsense. Philosophy is a flimsy foundation for theoretical rigour. But let's not get drawn into a discussion of the standards of philosophy. Consider instead the claim that a measure is rigorous if it is grounded in an 'accepted' philosophical theory.

Just about every philosophical theory is accepted by someone. Theories of happiness or wellbeing are no exception. Jeremy Bentham took subjective wellbeing to be a simple matter of pleasure and pain, measurable in 'hedons'. Others take it to be something more akin to contentment or whatever we might call the peaceful mental sunshine of the Dalai Lama. And there are several other contrary views of wellbeing that some people accept. Yet at most one of these accepted views is correct.

Acceptance is an absurdly weak standard for theoretical rigour. Any philosophical theory that is used as the ground for a measure of wellbeing is automatically accepted, at least by those so using it. You might as well define 'stylish clothes' as those that are worn by someone. No matter how hideous the clothes you wear, they will automatically pass this test for being stylish.

If a philosophy undergraduate wrote the quoted passage from Dolan et al., an examiner with any standards would give the essay a failing grade. Alas, it did not appear in an undergraduate's essay. It was written by academics considered to be among the world's leading thinkers on the topic of happiness policy, and it is to be found in a document published by a government toying with changing the tax code, the national curriculum for school pupils and much more in the hope of making us happier.

Now consider policy relevance, the second condition for a useful measure of wellbeing. This means that the measure is 'politically and socially acceptable, and also understood in policy circles'. This suffers from the same defect as their definition of theoretical rigour. A measure can easily be politically and socially acceptable, and understood in policy circles, without being correct. The science of phrenology was politically and socially acceptable in Germany in 1940. But measuring character, intelligence and other human qualities by the shape of the head and face was not made any more reliable by that fact.

Of course, this is not a test for reliability but for 'relevance'. Yet a false and unreliable theory must surely also be irrelevant in the sense of 'relevance' relevant to evidence-based policy. We are not here trying to win votes by appeal to irrational prejudice. We are trying to engineer public policy to achieve certain goals. In this context a theory is relevant only if it helps our engineering, which requires it to be true, not merely socially acceptable or understood in policy circles.

Few people in policy circles understand the techniques engineers use to measure the probability that a building will collapse in an earthquake. Does this make such measures irrelevant for setting building standards?

In a democracy the *policies* that result from all this happiness science might need to be socially acceptable, otherwise the politicians proposing them may lose votes and therefore be unable to carry them out. But the idea that the analysis of happiness on which these policies are based must itself be socially acceptable surely overestimates the intellectual tenacity of the average voter. I have read *Measuring Subjective Wellbeing for Public Policy*, but how many other voters will ever do so?

In short, these standards of rigour and relevance are sloppy and irrelevant. A measure of wellbeing that meets them should gain no credibility on account of that fact – if only because, as we have seen, almost any measure will meet these standards, no matter how bogus it is. I have spent some time on them only so that readers may get a sense of the intellectual standards being applied by Dolan et al. and the ONS.

The ONS measure is not empirically robust

Having specified that their account of wellbeing must be 'empirically robust' – that is, that it 'can be measured in a quantitative way that suggests that it is reliable and valid as an account of wellbeing' – Dolan et al. do not bother to show that their account meets this standard. This is strange. What is the point of specifying standards that your analysis must meet if you do not go on to show that it does in fact meet them? Never mind. It is easy to show that the account of happiness used by Dolan et al. and the ONS does not meet this standard.

Comparison and adaptivity

Empirically testable scientific theories allow us to measure the quantities they posit. For example, the relations between mass and force described by Newtonian physics allow us to build devices that measure mass. One way of doing this is to let the gravitational force exerted on an object placed on scales move a dial.

The more massive the object, the farther the dial will move and the greater the reading will be. In the same way, a mercury thermometer measures temperature by taking advantage of what we know about the rate at which mercury expands with temperature and, hence, the rate at which its level rises in a closed cylinder.

It is the hallmark of a rigorous empirical scientific theory that it allows for the precise measurement of the quantities it posits, such as mass, temperature, acidity, pressure and so on. Though these quantities are not directly observable – that is, observable by the unaided sense organs of us humans – the theory posits relationships between them and things that are directly observable, such as mercury rising in a closed cylinder or dials moving, which allow us to measure them.

What do we know about the observable effects of happiness that might allow us to measure it? According to Layard, some parts of our brain show more electrical activity or use more glucose when we do the things we say make us happy (see Layard, 2005: 17–20). Alas, this will not allow us to build a device for measuring happiness. For the theory linking happiness and brain activity is insufficiently well articulated. It is too rough and ready to allow us to 'read' happiness off brain activity. How much of which kind of brain activity equals how much happiness? Layard does not even suggest an answer.

This is the problem with most candidate measures of happiness. We know, for example, that people generally laugh and smile more when they are happy than when they are sad. But the connection is too loose and variable to provide a measure of happiness. People also smile and laugh when they are nervous, especially in some countries, such as Thailand. In other words, the 'folk-psychological' theory of which happiness is a concept is insufficiently precise about the relationships between happiness and directly observable phenomena to deliver a reliable measure of happiness.[3]

Happiness scientists have not tried to solve this problem in the way you might expect scientists to. They have not posited more precise and testable laws of happiness that might provide a basis for measuring it. Instead, they rely on people's assessment of their own happiness. 'How happy were you yesterday?' they ask. You reply, '7 out of 10', and you are registered as having been 7 out of 10 happy. What smiling and brain activity cannot deliver, self-reported happiness supposedly can. Dolan et al. and the ONS proceed on the assumption that self-reported happiness is a reliable measure of real happiness.

To see that this assumption is almost certainly wrong, suppose instead that I asked you how fat you are, on a scale of 0 to 10. Your answer will surely depend on how fat you are compared to what you deem to be your peer group. A 40-year-old woman whose body mass is 35 per cent fat might deem herself a 4 if she lives in New Orleans in 2013. If she lived there 100 years ago she would probably consider herself 7 or fatter. If she were a modern-day fashion model (unemployed, presumably), she would probably hate herself for being a 10.

This tendency to rate fatness by comparison with some peer group means that, if everyone in the group gets gradually fatter, its members will rate their fatness unchanged. If you were to measure the fatness of Americans by this method, you would massively

---

3   'Folk psychology' is a term used by philosophers of science to refer to the standard ideas we have about how people think and behave, especially the relationships between belief, desire and action. Just as 'mass' is a theoretical concept from Newtonian physics, so 'belief' and 'happiness' are theoretical concepts from folk psychology.

underestimate the extent to which they have become fatter over the last 50 years. Despite the average body fat percentage of adult women having risen steadily, most women will still rate themselves near to the median. It is not the number of women who are 5 out of 10 fat that changes but the fatness of the 5s.

Happiness is surely the same as fatness in this regard. Ask someone how happy he is and he will answer on the basis of some standard. That standard will be something like 'compared with people like me' or 'compared with what I might reasonably expect from life'. So, if everyone in his group gets happier or if what one might reasonably expect from life improves, self-assessed happiness will remain constant.

This may seem no more than obvious. Yet Layard and other happiness scientists claim to have discovered, on the basis of self-assessed happiness, that people have got no happier in the West as they have become richer and healthier, and that poor and insecure people in Nigeria are just as happy as safe and wealthy Germans (see Layard, 2005: 32).

According to Layard, getting more money does not make us happier because we adapt to it. Coming to take a certain level of wealth for granted, we no longer get as much happiness from it as we once would have. He illustrates this with the diagram overleaf (Figure 2).

Yet he has taken a liberty by representing the findings thus. What has really been shown is that *self-reported happiness* has not increased with increased wealth, that self-reported happiness is 'adaptive'. But, for the reasons given above, that is precisely what we would expect to observe even if real happiness were increasing. The additional car really has added to my happiness but, because my expected level of happiness has climbed, I rate my happiness

Figure 2   **Happiness adapts to consumption**

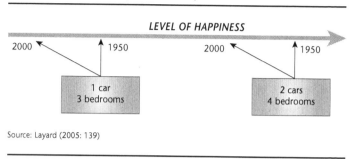

Source: Layard (2005: 139)

unchanged. This is represented in Figure 3, which distinguishes between real happiness and self-reported happiness.

Of course, this is probably a misrepresentation too. Real happiness probably is adaptive in the way that Layard suggests, at least to some extent. Owning two cars today probably does not cause as much real happiness as it would have 50 years ago. This is because owning two cars used to provide more social status than it does today, and status causes happiness.

But we cannot observe this adaptivity in the data collected by the ONS or previous studies because self-reported happiness is the only measure of happiness we have to go on, and it is adaptive with regard to real happiness. To put it another way, when we observe self-reported happiness adapting to circumstances, we do not know how much of this is due to the adaptivity of happiness to circumstances and how much is due to the adaptivity of self-reported happiness to real happiness.

We can discover how far fat-related standards have shifted over time, or how they vary between countries or subcultures, by comparing self-assessed fatness with objective measures of

Figure 3 **Self-reported happiness adapts to happiness**

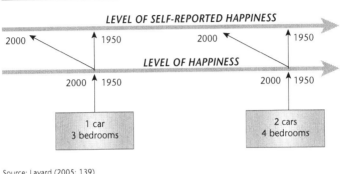

Source: Layard (2005: 139)

body fat. But we cannot do this for happiness because we have no measure of it except for the very reports of happiness that we are trying to calibrate to real happiness. We cannot know at what speed or with what perfection self-reported happiness adapts to real happiness because we have no independent purchase on real happiness. This renders the findings of what Layard calls the science of happiness more or less worthless. And the same goes for the findings of the ONS happiness survey, on which the government proposes to base public policy.

Caps and floors

A further peculiarity of the ONS measure of happiness is that it is bounded, imposing a maximum value of 10 and a minimum of 0. The measure is implicitly committed to the idea that there are levels of happiness and misery that cannot be exceeded.

Perhaps this is true. Perhaps there is a kind of cosmic bliss – achieved in Heaven or Nirvana or somewhere similarly glorious

– that is an upper bound to happiness. And perhaps Hell is the limit of misery. But these are not 'empirically robust' theses. The bounds of happiness and misery have not been identified by science. More importantly for the purposes of the ONS measure, it is obviously false that those who rate themselves a 10 or a 0 in happiness could not become yet happier or more miserable. The 10s among us are not evidence that Heaven really does exist on Earth.

These artificial bounds aggravate the problem created by the adaptivity of self-reported happiness. They mean that many real changes in happiness will not be identified by the measure. If something unexpectedly made everyone 20 per cent happier, the gains of those who were already 10s would not be counted at all, and the gains to the 9s would be understated, since moving from 9 to 10 is only an 11 per cent increase. The increase in average happiness would thus also be understated.

Given the adaptivity of self-reported happiness and the cramping effect of the upper and lower bounds of the ONS measure, I am willing to make a prediction about the average reported happiness of the British people over the coming decades; it will remain within ±0.5 points of its current 7.3.

The caps and floors imposed by the ONS measure are merely the most obvious source of distortion. The ONS reasons as if, between the bounds of 0 and 10, the relationship between self-reported happiness and real happiness is linear. For they report the average (mean) happiness within groups, such as UK citizens, men, people over 60 and so on. If you say you are 8 happy and I say I am 6, then the ONS says the average happiness of our little group is 7. Yet this follows only if your 8 signals 33 per cent more happiness than my 6. But why is this a safe assumption? Why

Figure 4   **Reported happiness versus real happiness**

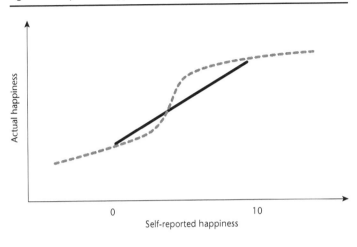

should we assume that self-reported happiness and real happiness stand in this linear relationship? Is someone who claims to be 6 happy really twice as happy as someone who claims to be 3 happy? For all the ONS knows, the shape of the relationship between self-reported and real happiness conforms not to the hard line in the chart above but to the dotted line.

The dotted line in Figure 4 is but one of many possible deviations from the linear relationship assumed by the ONS. Most are no less plausible than the ONS's linear model. Yet on any of them, the ONS's statistical analyses are wrong. For all the ONS knows, when you say you are 8 happy and I say I am 6, our mean happiness is not 7 but 6.5 or 7.5 or almost anything else in between 6 and 8.

Happiness is not a quantity

If the discussion above strikes you as foolish, that's because it is. For the sake of argument, I have followed the ONS in talking about happiness as if it resembles a physical quantity, such as mass or velocity, in being amenable to a measure that can properly be applied to quite different things. If I weigh 80kg and my wardrobe also weighs 80kg, as measured by standard scales, then the wardrobe and I really do have the same mass, despite our other differences.

But if you rate yourself 7 happy and I do too, are we equally happy? If I were to rate myself 3 yesterday and 6 today, have I really become twice as happy, and not only a third or quarter happier? Even if happiness were a genuine quantity, such as mass or velocity, it would be a miracle if this self-assessment measure gave equal readings for equal amounts of happiness (for the reasons already given). Yet the problem is more profound. Happiness surely is not a genuine quantity in the first place. Being in love, winning a race, seeing a child smile: these are all sources of happiness, as the term is ordinarily used. But the happiness produced by each is surely not a single quantity, in a way that would allow my happiness (caused by seeing a child smile, let's say) and your happiness (caused by winning a race) to be assigned numbers that properly belong on a single scale and that can therefore be summed, averaged and so on.

As Layard correctly points out, 'there are many different sources of noise, from a trombone to a pneumatic drill, but we can feel how loud each noise is' (Layard, 2005: 13). Indeed, we can do even better than *feel* how loud noises are; we can measure their volumes in decibels. But this does not show that happiness really is a quantity after all. Of course, quite different things *can* exemplify the same quantity, in the way that different noises can all have a volume, measurable in decibels, or different objects can all have a mass, measurable in kilograms. But it does not follow from the fact that some terms, such as 'mass' and 'volume', refer to real quantities that all of them do.

We may be able to rank our happiness from day to day; we may have a rough idea of what makes us happy; and we may even know which bits of our brains are active when we are happy. But it does not follow from any or all of this that happiness is a genuine quantity. The reason Layard, the ONS and the rest have failed to come up with a measure of happiness fit for scientific use is not that they are incompetent; it is that happiness simply is not amenable to this kind of measurement. The prime minister gave the ONS an impossible job.

The same impossibility would arise for measuring most of the concepts of 'folk psychology'. Consider love, for example. We will never get a measure of love, equally applicable to all the love felt by everyone, which will allow us to determine the average love felt by Britons and to distil 'lessons from the new science of love'. This is because love varies not only in its causes but in what it is. There can be no measure that applies equally to an 80-year-old woman's love for her cat and a 17-year-old boy's love for his girlfriend. These are not different amounts of the same kind of thing; they are different kinds of thing. Many of the different feelings we have are similar enough to warrant calling all of them 'love', and we may even be able to rank our feelings of love by their intensity or longevity or whatever. But that does not mean that love is a genuine quantity, amenable to a single measure for all its instances.

Dolan et al. and the ONS officials who accepted their advice show a peculiar ignorance of the history of ideas. Jeremy Bentham and his utilitarian followers also believed that public policy should aim at maximising national happiness. They understood that this required happiness or 'utility' to be a genuine quantity. They even coined the expression 'hedon' for the unit of happiness: the equivalent of kilogrammes for mass or decibels for volume. Alas, their theory of happiness was insufficiently rigorous to deliver on this terminological promise; they could not provide a way of measuring hedons. Benthamite utilitarianism ultimately foundered on this failure.

If you wish to resurrect Benthamite utilitarianism – as Layard and, by association, Cameron do – then *this* is your intellectual challenge.[4] You must show that happiness really is a quantity and that you have discovered a measure of it, each of whose numeric readings signals the same amount of happiness no matter to whom or when the measure is applied. Yet no such advance has been made on the failed efforts of Bentham and his followers. Layard and the ONS certainly provide no such measure. Instead they pretend that they can found their 'scientific' inquiries and coercive public policy proposals on a survey of self-assessed happiness. It would be funny if only the history of tyranny were not so intimately associated with the history of bogus science.

Preferences and happiness

The science of happiness is too flimsy to be the proper foundation of a programme of social engineering. Indeed, if we take the term

---

4   Layard is explicit about wishing to pursue Jeremy Bentham's ideas (see Layard, 2005: 4–6). Cameron is probably less aware of the ideas he is effectively signing up to.

'science' seriously, then there is no science of happiness. That is what I have argued so far. But even if the science of happiness were sound, it would not follow that public policy should be aimed at maximising happiness. What is so good about happiness?

Neither Layard nor Cameron even try to answer the question. This displays a remarkably cavalier attitude considering that they propose using state coercion for the purpose of maximising happiness and considering the long history of failure by great thinkers, including John Stuart Mill, to justify giving the pursuit of happiness this pre-eminence in our lives.[5]

It is not difficult to show that public policy should not be aimed at making us happy. The reason is that happiness is but one of many scarce goods. And, as with anything else, the optimal trade-off between happiness and other goods varies from individual to individual and from time to time, depending on factors far better known to the individuals concerned than to government officials. Most obviously, it depends on the individuals' preferences regarding happiness and other goods.

Consider a simple example. Suppose I want a bespoke suit made by a Savile Row tailor that will cost £4,000. I have the opportunity to work 200 hours of overtime at £20 an hour and to thereby save the required money. I also want to be happy, however, and I have learnt from Layard that swapping leisure for work will make me less happy. Should I do the overtime and trade some happiness for the suit? Or should I forgo the overtime and the suit for the sake of the happiness I keep?

The answer depends, of course, on which I prefer: the

---

5   John Stuart Mill's notoriously bad argument for why maximising aggregate happiness should be the goal of human action can be found in Chapter 3 of his *Utilitarianism* (Mill, 1863).

happiness or the suit. I can know which I prefer but neither Layard nor Cameron can know, and nor can any other stranger. So policies that aim to make me forgo the overtime-earned suit for the sake of the leisure-induced happiness – such as heavily taxing my overtime pay, as Layard recommends – may well harm me. For all the authorities know, I may prefer the suit to the happiness.

Some will think I am talking nonsense here. If someone wants a Savile Row suit, that is surely because he thinks it will make him happy. The above trade-off between the leisure and the suit is really a trade-off between different sources of happiness. And my goal is to make the trade-off which maximises my happiness.

The idea that all our actions are ultimately aimed at happiness is remarkably common. I suspect it explains why Layard, Cameron and other happiness merchants do not waste a moment on explaining why happiness is the proper goal of government policy. They simply take it for granted that our ultimate goal is happiness. We often fail to achieve happiness, they believe, only because we do not understand its causes or are subject to irrational impulses or to unhappy external forces – from all of which the government, armed with Layard's new science, can relieve us.

Despite its popularity, the idea that all our trade-offs seek to maximise happiness is wrong. Depending on what is meant by 'happiness', it is either a mere tautology with no implications for public policy or it is obviously false.

Start with the tautological interpretation. Suppose 'happy' is used to refer not to any particular mental state, such as the quiet mental glow of the Dalai Lama or the exhilaration of infatuation or whatever, but merely to the satisfaction of your preferences, to getting what you want. Then it is trivially true that people seek only happiness. I prefer the suit to the leisure, so I do the overtime and get the suit. This is my preferred and, hence, my happy trade-off. You prefer the leisure to the suit. So you do not do the overtime. That is therefore your happy trade-off. A politician seeking to maximise happiness, thus understood, will aim to maximise preference satisfaction, with no particular view as to what those preferences should be. He will not promote leisure over work, nor encourage communal solidarity by restricting freedom of movement, nor ban adverts that give people preferences unconducive to happiness (a notion which makes no sense on this interpretation of 'happy'). In short, if you interpret happiness as preference satisfaction, then, though people are by definition guaranteed always to seek happiness, you are left without a distinctive policy agenda. Happiness policies are simply those that allow people to pursue their own interests as they see them: that is, happiness policies are laissez-faire policies.

Of course, this is not how Layard, Cameron and the rest interpret happiness, and they certainly do not have a laissez-faire policy agenda. On the contrary, they believe the state should coerce people to act against their preferences in ways that will make them happier.

But once you conceive of happiness as some particular mental state, as being something other than simple preference satisfaction, then it is obviously false that people seek to maximise their happiness, even 'ultimately'. Suppose, for example, that we identify happiness with the Dalai Lama's famously contented mental state – measurable, let's pretend, in Lamons. I know that many of the things I want will not increase my Lamons: a Savile Row suit will not, a mansion on Hampstead Heath will not, the flattery of beautiful women will not. Nevertheless, I want these things. Indeed, I would gladly trade some Lamons for them.

The point does not depend on the particular Lamonic conception of happiness being used. On any non-trivial conception of happiness, many of our preferences are not happiness-seeking. A man may genuinely seek glory or truth or a Ferrari without believing that it will make him happy. He simply wants it.

Of course, Layard and Cameron will think this man is making a mistake, and that I am foolish to trade Lamons for my vanities. But what kind of a mistake is it? Where do they think I have erred?

Not in misapprehending my own preferences. Even they surely cannot think they know my preferences better than I do. No, they must think that I have misapprehended the objective fact that happiness is the proper end of human action. My preferences are based on values that do not match the true, objective values of things. I rate a Savile Row suit higher than the little bit of happiness I must forgo for it. But, as a matter of objective fact, that extra little bit of happiness is worth more than the Savile Row suit. Layard and Cameron may not know what I want, but they do know what is good for me.

Those who believe the government should design public policy to maximise national happiness are not simply utilitarians; they fall into a particular camp of utilitarianism: they are so-called list utilitarians.

A list utilitarian is best understood by contrast with a 'preference utilitarian'. A preference utilitarian equates utility or personal welfare with preference satisfaction.[6] This is the position

---

6   This is a slight simplification but the subtleties of preference utilitarianism do not matter for current purposes. What I am calling 'preference utilitarianism' is now mainstream thought in welfare economics.

sketched above, when happiness was equated with preference satisfaction. Preference utilitarians have no particular conception of utility or welfare. What counts as the 'good life' or utility maximisation depends on what people want. The overtime-funded suit might maximise my welfare while the happy leisure maximises yours. Preference utilitarianism encourages laissez-faire policy.

A list utilitarian, by contrast, has a particular conception of welfare or utility or 'what is good for people'. He believes he can list the features of the good life: hence, 'list utilitarianism'. Layard and Cameron are list utilitarians with a very short, one-item list. The good life is the happy life. And the happier your life, the better it is.

Though they might reject the 'utilitarian' title, the economist Amartya Sen and philosopher Martha Nussbaum are also listers. They claim to know the features of the good life and demand that governments devote themselves to providing citizens with the 'capabilities' required to achieve such good lives.[7] According to Nussbaum, the ten proper goals of government policy are: life; bodily health; bodily integrity; senses, imagination and thought (that's one capability); emotions; practical reason; affiliation; other species; play; and control over one's environment (Nussbaum, 2000).

The economic historian Lord Robert Skidelsky and his son, the philosopher Edward Skidelsky, are also listers. In their recently published *How Much Is Enough?* they claim the good life has seven elements and that governments should devote themselves to ensuring citizens get enough of them, whether they want

---

7   The scholarly work of Sen and Nussbaum has inspired a capabilities-based approach to welfare that is increasingly popular with other academics and with development agencies.

them or not (see Skidelsky and Skidelsky, 2012). These seven goods are health, security, friendship, leisure, personality, respect, and Savile Row suits. No, only joking: not Savile Row suits, harmony with nature.

But, joking aside, why are Savile Row suits less important than harmony with nature or leisure or all the other things on the Skidelskys' list? The Skidelskys provide no empirical evidence that leisure is objectively more valuable than a nice suit (how could they?) nor any valid argument for this conclusion from obviously true premises (again, how could they?). Their list is compiled simply from their own judgements about what really matters in life – judgements that they ask us to believe are a more reliable guide to the true, objective values than are the judgements of us dissenters.

Listers display heroic moral confidence. Set aside for a moment the contempt the likes of Layard, Nussbaum and Skidelsky show for the actual preferences of ordinary people. They can surely see that they disagree with each other. Lord Skidelsky can see that Lord Layard disagrees with him about what is on the list of ultimate goods that people should be coerced to pursue. Yet he does not pause to doubt the reliability of his moral intuitions. He concludes that his moral sensibilities are so exalted that even the contrary opinions of another high-minded and scholarly lord are to be dismissed as failures of moral apprehension. And vice versa. Lord Layard must think that, like the rest of us who do not rate happiness the be-all and end-all of human life, Lord Skidelsky is morally benighted. If either lord could win the day, he would tax and otherwise coerce his intellectual rivals into living according to his moral vision.

Layard claims that directing public policy towards maximising happiness is 'fundamentally egalitarian because everybody's happiness is to count equally' (Layard, 2005: 5). This reveals an extraordinary idea of political equality. Imagine the government devoted itself to maximising the size of the population and, to this end, taxed people who did not reproduce with sufficient regularity, encouraged sex without contraception in school lessons and took the other kinds of measures that Layard recommends in the pursuit of happiness. This would be egalitarian by Layard's reasoning because when measuring population growth, everyone would be counted equally. Never mind that much of the population would be coerced into living according to values that they reject. They are treated equally because the officials imposing the reproductive priority on them count them the same as people who would pursue reproduction voluntarily.

Layard's proposed policy regime, in which people are taxed, 'educated' and otherwise corralled into pursuing happiness, is, in fact, the antithesis of egalitarian. It involves the coercive replacement of citizens' values with Layard's values. The same goes for all the other listers' proposed regimes. The equality of citizens would be reduced to little more than equality among slaves – or, if you prefer, equality among the children of authoritarian parents.

Of the four evidence-based policies considered in this book, the happiness agenda of Layard and Cameron is the most outrageous example of intellectual and political hubris. Because everything can affect our happiness, it suggests no limit on government action. Yet it is based on shoddy philosophy, simply ignoring the problems on which Benthamite utilitarianism foundered, and on even worse 'science'. The survey-based self-assessment measure of happiness is so unreliable that anyone who takes seriously the 'lessons of the new science' displays remarkable credulity.

Or opportunism. Many people seek to replace your preferences and decisions with their own. They do not necessarily seek material gain. They may simply be overwhelmed by an exaggerated sense of their own morality and wisdom: 'if only others acted by the light of my wisdom, the world would be such a wonderful place!' Whatever their motivation, such people are always on the lookout for the latest 'scientific breakthrough' that appears to justify their meddling. They are primed for credulity. The rest of us, the proposed meddlees, are well advised to remain sceptical.

6 SCIENTIFIC AUTHORITY

Parliamentarians and parents have authority. If someone asks why it is illegal in Britain to pay someone less than £6 for an hour's work or to speak hatefully about religious people, the correct answer is simply that Parliament has declared it so. Parliament is a legal authority – quite literally, the author of our laws. Similarly, when my daughter asks why her bedtime is 8 p.m. and I answer 'because I say so', despite her protests, I am making no mistake. On this matter, I am an authority; I simply cannot be wrong about my daughter's bedtime because I create it by declaring it.[1]

Scientists lack authority. Light bends under gravitational force. But not because Albert Einstein said it does. Einstein was not the author of this fact. He discovered it. That is why our going along with his idea requires more than his say-so. We need evidence, such as that provided by Sir Arthur Eddington's observations during a 1919 solar eclipse, which showed the light from distant stars bending around the gravitational field of the Sun, as Einstein's theory predicted it would. The same goes for all scientific inquiry. It aims to discover facts that are not matters of convention and are therefore independent of human decree and authority.

---

1   I also need to show a genuine willingness to enforce my little law. If I never punish my daughter for going to bed after 8 p.m., and no convention of going to bed at this time is established then, despite what I say, 8 p.m. is not really her bedtime. See, for example, Hart (1961).

Yet someone following contemporary debates about public policy might be forgiven for having doubts. Scientists are constantly being put forward as authorities on the issues under dispute. Why should you believe that a minimum price for alcohol will benefit the people of Britain? Because Dr Ian Gilmore, a professor of medicine, says it will, as do the representatives of august scientific bodies, such as the British Medical Association and the Royal College of Physicians. Why should you believe that carbon emissions, if unchecked, will cause an environmental disaster? Because 90 per cent of scientists surveyed say they will – and so on. Despite the absence of authority in science, we are expected to defer to scientists.

And rightly so, up to a point. For, in an extended sense of the word, scientists *are* authorities on the topics of their research: in the sense, that is, of being experts. This expertise warrants deference on the part of non-experts. But the warranted deference to scientists is more sceptical and constrained than politicians, journalists and lobbyists – often including the scientists themselves – would have us believe. On matters where respect for the opinions of scientists is said to 'end the debate', those opinions are often owed less than the suggested level of respect. Explaining why is the purpose of this chapter.

Reliability and degrees of belief

People often talk about science as if it were a single discipline ('science has shown', 'scientists believe') with a single method ('the scientific method') and all scientifically acquired beliefs were therefore equally likely to be true and equally credible.

This vision of science is entirely wrong. Scientific inquiry encompasses a great variety of disciplines, with different methods, some of which are more reliable than others. Particle physics, evolutionary biology, epidemiology, climatology and behavioural economics, to take but five examples, concern different phenomena, use different methods and produce results of very different credibility. Expert practitioners in one of these fields may be quite ignorant of the other fields, knowing little about either their theories or their methods.

Nor do sciences provide the only reliable ways of forming true opinions. I am writing this sentence while sitting in a café in Brussels. I believe I am in Brussels on the basis of no scientific theory or scientific method. I got the belief in a much more everyday way, relying on my ability to see, to read, to remember and so on. Yet the chance that this belief of mine is wrong is tiny: far smaller than the chance that the current theories of climatology or cosmology are wrong.

My point here is not to disparage the latest theories of climatology or cosmology. On the matters they concern, they probably provide our best chance of knowing the truth. Rather, my point is that what we care about – or, at least, what we should care about – is reliability. Given the way I arrived at my belief, how likely is it to be true? This is the question that should concern the earnest truth-seeker. And the simple distinction between scientific and unscientific ways of forming beliefs is not helpful in this regard. Some unscientific ways of arriving at beliefs are reliable and some scientific ways are unreliable.

Just as our ways of arriving at beliefs vary in their reliability, so our beliefs vary in the degree of confidence with which we hold them. I believe that President Obama was born in Hawaii. But I believe this with less confidence or certainty than I believe that I am now sitting in a café in Brussels. In other words, belief comes by degree, ranging from 1 (complete certainty) down to 0 (complete disbelief or certainty of falsity).[2]

A rational man will make his degree of belief the same as the reliability of the way it was acquired. To illustrate, suppose that I have tossed a coin and placed my hand over it. To what degree should you believe that it landed heads? Since my hand prevents you from seeing whether it is heads or tails, and its landing heads had a chance of 0.5, your degree of belief that it is heads ought to be 0.5 (and also 0.5 that it is tails). The reliability of guessing an outcome is equal to the probability of the outcome. So your degree of belief in guesses should be the same as the probability of what is guessed.

But now suppose I lift my hand and you see that it is heads. Now your degree of belief that it is heads ought to rise to almost 1, because looking at coins is an almost perfectly reliable way of arriving at the belief that they landed heads (assuming your eyes are healthy, the light is good, you are close enough and so on). When you look at a coin under the right circumstances, and come to believe that it is heads-up, then the probability that it is heads-up is very close to 1.

The same goes for science. Scientists ought to let the confidence with which they hold their beliefs vary with the reliability

---

2   It is unlikely anyone is completely certain of anything. I, for one, can think of no proposition on which I would accept the following odds: one penny if I am right versus everlasting damnation if I am wrong. I would not accept these odds even on the proposition that I am in Brussels. Maybe I am actually in a London hospital, unwittingly taking part in an experiment on my brain. But for practical purposes, my degree of belief in this proposition, and many others, is close enough to 1 as makes no difference. So I shall set aside such 'metaphysical doubt' in this chapter.

of the way they arrived at them: that is, with the chance that their beliefs are true given the way they got them. The physics of medium-sized objects moving at velocities well below the speed of light has been experimentally tested and successfully applied in technology to such an extent that it is beyond reasonable doubt. The proper degree of belief in basic physics and its predictions is near to 1. Climatology, by contrast, does not warrant such confidence. Its long-term predictions have not been tested and its short-term predictions are frequently wrong. A climatologist ought to doubt his preferred theory and the predictions that issue from it; his degrees of belief ought to be well shy of 1. The same goes for the latest theories in most fields of ongoing scientific inquiry, such as happiness, sociobiology, macroeconomics, neurolinguistics and many-worlds quantum mechanics. Inquiry is ongoing precisely because near-certainty has not been achieved.

Deference and certification

Now consider the position of a layman with respect to some scientific theory. He knows neither the details of the theory nor how well it has been confirmed by experiments or other observations. So he cannot judge its credibility. In these circumstances, to what degree should he believe the theory and its predictions?

The simple answer is that he must defer to scientists working in the field. Unlike the layman, these experts do understand the theory and how well confirmed it is. So the layman should simply follow the scientist. The layman's degree of belief should be the same as the scientist's.

For reasons I will give below, this is not always true. Laymen are often wise to have a lower degree of belief in a theory and its predictions than scientists who work in the field, especially when those scientists are contributing their views to a policy debate. But first we need to understand better the logic and practical requirements of intellectual deference.

I say 'intellectual deference' rather than 'scientific deference' because, again, the distinction between scientific and unscientific ways of acquiring beliefs is irrelevant to the logic of deference. We get many of our beliefs by deferring to people who are not scientists. For example, you probably have various beliefs about your mother's childhood: about where she lived, where she went to school and much besides. You did not get these beliefs by observing your mother as a girl: you got them from what your mother and others told you about her childhood and, perhaps, from photos. Similarly, your beliefs about places you have not visited, times you have not lived in and people you have not met are acquired by deferring to the opinions of others: to what they write in history books or show you on TV or tell you in confidence or otherwise communicate.

Deference is simply another way in which we get beliefs. I can believe you were in the pub last night because I saw you there or because someone told me you were there. Which of these two ways of getting the belief inspires the greater confidence in me will depend on how reliable I take it to be. Seeing things for myself will normally beat reports of them, but it need not. If I was blind drunk and the room was dark, then relying on what I saw is probably more likely to lead to error than relying on the testimony of my witness, assuming he was sober and has no reason to lie.

When it comes to most fields of science, most of us are in the dark. So we are wise to defer to those who know more than we do:

that is, to the experts in the field. But who are the experts? This is the first problem for us would-be deferrers.

When it comes to our friends and relatives, we know enough about them to have a fair idea of how far to trust their opinions on various topics. Alas, we usually do not personally know the scientists whose opinions we must defer to. So, instead, we rely on certification. Some people are certified as reliable sources on certain topics. The most obvious forms of certification are academic qualifications, employment in academic positions at reputable universities and membership of scholarly or professional bodies, such as the Royal Society or the British Medical Association. These are the people whose specialist beliefs you should defer to.

Nor is it only people that get this kind of certification. Some of their beliefs are also certified. An idea that has been published in a peer-reviewed journal article is commonly deemed to be more dependable than one that has not. And some ideas get official certification from scientific reports commissioned by governmental agencies. The reports of the Intergovernmental Panel on Climate Change (IPCC) are exemplars of this kind of double certification: certified ideas from certified people.

So the quick answer to the question 'to what degree should I believe the claims of scientific theories that I cannot evaluate?' is this: believe them to the same degree as the certified experts in the field. But this quick answer is too quick, for the following reasons.

Concealed doubt

In economics, psychology and philosophy it is uncontentious that belief comes by degrees. But many people – including politicians, cult leaders, quack doctors and campaigning journalists – speak as if belief were either all-on or all-off, as if you either believe something or you do not.

Those in the business of selling their opinions are naturally reluctant to admit to doubt. 'Follow me, brother, for I know the path to salvation!' This might convince some people to follow you or even to fund your journey. 'Follow me, brother, for I want to take a path that I am fairly confident leads to salvation.' That isn't such a compelling sales pitch.

Scientists are not supposed to be in the business of selling their opinions; they are not politicians or journalists or cult leaders. They are supposed to be in the business of discovering the truth. Yet, when it comes to scientific contributions to public policy debate, it is difficult to discover the doubts of scientists working in the relevant field. We are told only that, after considering all the evidence, on balance, scientists believe such and such. But this is not what interested laymen and, especially, policymakers need to know. They need to know *the degree to which* the certified scientists believe the thesis concerned.

If their degree of belief were less than 0.5, then the simple claim to believe the thesis would amount to a lie. After all, these scientists would be more confident that the thesis was false. So, outright dishonesty aside, we may assume that when a scientist declares belief, his degree of belief exceeds 0.5. But this may not be enough for laymen considering acting on scientists' beliefs.

Suppose you are a keen cheese-eater. You read in the newspaper that scientists have discovered that eating cheese doubles the chance of suffering a heart attack. Should you quit eating cheese? That will depend on several things, including your age, the value you place on living, your initial chance of a heart attack, your love of cheese *and the degree to which you believe the purported discovery*. Suppose that, given all the other factors, you will quit cheese only if your confidence in the alleged discovery is 0.75 or more. Then you will not know what to do. You know only that the certified scientists to whom you wish to defer believe that cheese doubles the chance of a heart attack with a degree of confidence exceeding 0.5. You do not know whether it exceeds your 0.75 threshold for quitting.

When scientists communicate their findings to the public and politicians, they rarely mention the warranted degree of belief, not even with a simple 1 to 5 confidence scale or something similar.[3] For all their audience knows, the warranted degree of belief is anywhere between 0.5 and 1. Different values within that range can have quite different implications for what is the right action or policy. Alas, those untutored in the fact that belief comes by degree will be inclined to interpret these unqualified declarations of belief as meaning that scientists are certain. That is to say, they will reason as if the proper degree of belief in the proposition is 1. Since this will rarely be true, especially on contentious matters, they will often be led into error by such simple statements of scientific belief.

The fashion for letters to the editor declaring the 'scientific consensus' on various matters of public concern, signed by dozens or even hundreds of scientists, reinforces the common misapprehension that the assertions of scientists signify degrees of belief close to 1. For these letters make sense only on this incorrect supposition.

---

3   The reports of the Intergovernmental Panel on Climate Change do assign confidence levels to some of their assertions (see Chapter 4). This is commendable. Alas, the use made of these reports by activists, journalists and politicians rarely takes any account of the confidence levels specified. What's more, for reasons given later in this section, we should be sceptical about the stated confidence levels.

To see why, start by asking why the large number of signatories should help to convince readers of the truth of the letter's content. The answer must be that the signatories are implicitly invoking a statistical argument for deferring to them. 'We the undersigned, *who are a majority of certified scientists in the field*, believe such and such. So you, inexpert reader, should believe it too.'

Accept for a moment that the implicit appeal to the average (mean) belief of certified scientists provides a sensible ground for deference. Suppose the undersigned constitute 75 per cent of certified scientists. Then their belief in the thesis concerned guarantees an average degree of belief greater than 0.5 in *all* certified scientists only if the average degree of belief among the signatories exceeds 0.67. Or, to put it the other way around, if the 25 per cent of dissenting experts have a 0 degree of belief, then the average will be under 0.5 if the 75 per cent believe with less than 0.67 confidence. But the 'undersigned' 75 per cent – or whatever percentage they are, which they cannot actually know – never specify their degree of belief. They simply declare belief, relying on readers' assumption that this signifies certainty. If they were open about their degrees of belief, the letter would lose any vestige of logical coherence and, with it, any persuasive force.

Many of the undersigned may do this out of honest ignorance. They may not know how strongly they believe what they are declaring. Until confronted with a genuine wager on something, it can be difficult to know the degree to which you believe it. And genuine wagers are often difficult to arrange on the truth of scientific theories or their predictions for the far-off future. There is no obvious or timely test for being right.

Scientists may also fail to mention their degree of belief

because they do not understand its importance. The undersigned may not know that the proper policy response to the claims they are making depends on the confidence with which they are believed. Climatologists, epidemiologists and other non-economists usually know little about decision theory. Many do not understand that, when it comes to deciding what to do on the basis of believing something, there is a world of difference between having a 0.99 degree of belief and a 0.51 degree.

But the more likely explanation for concealing scientific doubt is what has come to be known as noble-cause corruption (see Chapter 3). Return to the cheese example. You will give up cheese only if you have a 0.75 degree of belief that cheese doubles your chance of a heart attack. Suppose this is because you have an unusually powerful love of cheese and a peculiar lack of concern for ill-health and premature death.

Your doctor may well lament these values. Doctors often wish people cared more for their health, and they see it as part of their job to get people to lead healthier lives. Your doctor will find it difficult to make you like cheese less than you do or to care more for your health. But, since you defer to him on medical matters of fact, he can get you to change your degrees of belief. By raising your degree of belief that cheese doubles the chance of a heart attack above your 0.75 threshold, he can get you to give up cheese. In his view, he will be helping you, even if the warranted degree of belief is only 0.6. He is more concerned that you adopt healthy habits than that you have the proper degree of belief in medical theses. In short, your doctor's priorities, when they differ from yours, tempt him to mislead you, to tell you that the cheese 'discovery' warrants more confidence than it really does.

The same goes for scientists working on topics of relevance to public policy. A scientist working on the health effects of passive smoking may have preferences regarding health, the experience of inhaling smoke and so on which mean that, *if everyone shared his preferences*, the world would be better if no one smoked in enclosed public spaces. But that italicised qualification may not occur to him or he may see the preferences of those who voluntarily visit smoky pubs as simply mistaken: that is, he may be a 'list utilitarian', if only unconsciously (see Chapter 5). If his contribution to public debate causes people with the wrong values to overestimate the credibility of theses about the harm caused by passive smoking, he will see himself as helping to improve public policy. And giving in to this temptation is easy because it can be done in ways that do not force the corruption into his consciousness. When he says that 'the vast majority of scientists believe ...' he has not strictly lied; he has merely said something that is likely to be misunderstood in a way that promotes actions he happens to support.

For this reason, lay people should discount the claims of scientists working in fields relevant to public policy. The temptation to exaggerate confidence is especially acute in fields that have long been policy battlegrounds, such as climate, health and education. Many scientists working in such fields entered them precisely because they were already committed to a policy agenda for which they wanted to provide factual support, or because they wanted to provide scientific grounds for rejecting it. This fact should be irrelevant to the scientific colleagues of these 'motivated inquirers' (see Chapter 3). Scientists rely not on trust but on evidence and argument. But it does justify scepticism in laymen who, not knowing the evidence and arguments, do rely on trust. They must know who they should defer to, and with how much confidence.

Motivations for exaggeration among the experts are grounds for scepticism among laymen.

Certification is not additional evidence

The certification of scientists by formal qualifications, university employment and the rest is useful for laymen. It helps us to identify those we should defer to. Yet, just as the certified scientists' simple statements of belief can mislead laymen, so can the certification itself. It can suggest that there is some common standard of scientific rigour and credibility met by the work of all certified scientists. There is not.

Consider the PhD degree. A PhD can be earned in almost any subject, from particle physics to anthropology to literary criticism. That someone possesses a PhD tells you little about the credence due to his various declarations. All you know is that he has met the standard for earning this degree in his field of study. And that may be a standard that lends little credibility to his statements. In some cases, this is because the field is a swamp. Someone who has gone through the intellectual process required to get a PhD in post-structuralist literary criticism or some of the more politicised branches of sociology, for example, will probably have reduced his chance of uttering truths: he will have corrupted his mind. You should be less inclined to believe what he has to say on his chosen field – what poems mean, why people live as they do, and so on – than to hold on to your initial, untutored opinions.

But the subjects that unquestionably qualify as sciences are not intellectual swamps. Someone with a PhD in physics or chemistry or oncology or climate change is likely to know far more about the subject than someone without a PhD. Nevertheless, the chance that their opinions are true may remain low. No matter how clever someone is, no matter how rigorous his mathematical modelling or theoretical reasoning, he cannot overcome an inability to test empirical hypotheses. For example, no intellectual virtue can compensate for the fact that the long-term predictions of climate models have not been tested. Nor can macroeconomics overcome the near-impossibility of conducting controlled and repeatable experiments.

A student can understand the latest theories in his field, and make a contribution to them that rightly earns him a PhD. But he remains a no more reliable source than is allowed by his subject. Someone who earns a PhD in climatology may be more brilliant than someone who earns one in chemistry. Nevertheless, his predictions about the climate remain less dependable than the chemist's predictions about reactions.

The same goes for the 'peer review' of academic articles. At best, this shows that an article meets the standards of the academic field concerned.[4] It tells you nothing about the standards of that field, the reliability of the methods used or the credibility of the conclusions arrived at. Even the articles in post-structuralist literary criticism journals are peer-reviewed. Someone who rejects the conclusions of a peer-reviewed article is not guaranteed to be wrong, if only because, in most fields, there will be some other peer-reviewed article that also rejects them.

Expertise slippage

Laymen must also beware what I call 'expertise slippage': that is, the tendency to defer to experts on matters that fall outside

---

4   At worst, it shows that the carefully selected referees are already well disposed towards the conclusions drawn in the article.

their field of expertise. This happens most obviously where intellectual superstars are concerned. For example, many people are impressed by what Stephen Hawking has to say about the old philosophical problem of how (or whether) people can have free will in a deterministic universe. Yet he has no expertise in philosophy and his comments on the topic would not achieve a high grade for an undergraduate philosophy student. People listen to his philosophical ideas only because he is a great physicist.

Similarly, many people have told me that humans use only 10 per cent of their mental capabilities. When I ask them why they believe this, they usually tell me that Einstein said so. But so what? Einstein was a physicist, not a psychologist. He was no more likely to be right than any other reasonable person about how much of our mental capacity we use. In fact, his own extraordinary intelligence may have inclined him generally to overestimate people's mental capabilities.

On matters of public policy, expertise slippage takes a characteristic form. Politicians, journalists and lobbyists appear to believe that if a policy concerns something, such as health or education or livestock, then people who work in those areas – doctors, teachers and farmers – are the relevant experts on the policy. This is usually a mistake.

To see why, consider again Professor Sir Ian Gilmore's 2010 demand that the government adopt his evidence-based policy of imposing a minimum price for a unit of alcohol (see Chapter 2). Professor Gilmore was to be found on television and quoted in newspaper articles. He was presented to his political and general audiences as an expert on the matter at hand, as someone properly qualified to tell us that the minimum alcohol price is a good public policy.

Professor Gilmore is a medical scientist. He probably understands the health effects of alcohol very well. But, as we saw in Chapter 2, the health effects of alcohol cannot justify the policy. The serious questions raised by the policy concern welfare economics, a subject on which Professor Gilmore apparently has no expertise at all. His expertise in medical matters has caused him to be treated as an authority on a subject where he lacks the relevant expertise. That is expertise slippage.

Or consider the debate over carbon emissions and policies to restrict them. The support of climate scientists for some such policy is often presented as grounds for laymen also to support the policy. But climate scientists are experts on hardly any of the issues that determine which climate policies are best. Perhaps they understand the relationship between carbon emissions and air temperatures. But they have no special knowledge of how businesses will respond to taxes, the likelihood of compliance with international treaties, the relative welfare costs of reduced growth and so on. On most of what matters for climate policy, a climate scientist knows no more than those who defer to them. You might as well treat an engineer who designs battleships as an expert on defence policy or a farmer as an expert on agricultural policy. It is an absurd mistake but no less common for that.

Scientists are interested parties

Besides their ignorance on the relevant issues, deferring to a farmer on agricultural policy or a battleship engineer on defence policy is a mistake because farmers and battleship engineers are interested parties. They stand to gain from policy taking one direction rather than another. So they will be tempted to support the personally profitable policy direction, even if they understand that it is altogether harmful.

The same goes for scientists. Public policy can create demand for their skills and hence drive up the rewards accruing to them. Consider again the kind of mathematical risk-measurement techniques that have been developed over recent decades (discussed in Chapters 2 and 4). In 2001 the Basel Committee, which formulates international banking regulation, decided that (from 2007) banks that use these techniques would be allowed to hold lower levels of equity capital than banks that used rules of thumb to estimate risk. This created an employment boom for people with the relevant skills as banks scrambled to comply with this regulation. It also made the experts in these techniques keen supporters of the Basel regulations. And not just keen but effective supporters. To whom should policymakers turn for advice when devising rules that will make banks safe? To these experts on mathematical risk modelling, of course!

Experts are natural supporters of policies that draw on their expertise and thus naturally inclined to overstate the credibility and importance of their ideas. When you ask a macroeconomist about the reliability of macroeconomic forecasting, do you expect him to understate or overstate his subject's achievements? When you ask a climate scientist about the likelihood of catastrophic global warming, do you expect him to understate or overstate the risk? Do you expect doctors to tell you that, considering that life is short and often bleak, people should not worry too much about their health but instead eat, drink and be merry?

We are rightly sceptical when a businessman asks us to take his word for something if he benefits from our believing it. Well, scientists are only human and they need to make a living too.

When a scientist asks us to believe something that will elevate his social status or increase the demand for his labour, we are wise to believe it with less confidence than he appears to.

The issue in perfect miniature: Kahneman on anthropogenic global warming

As noted above, when deferring to our friends and families about supposed matters of fact, we often 'discount' their degrees of belief. If my aunt tells me she is certain that my nephew is planning to leave his wife, I may come to believe it too but I won't be as certain as she is. On such matters, my aunt is not a perfectly reliable source. The same goes for our deference to scientists. We are inclined to discount our deference to those we deem unreliable on the subject at hand. Politicians and campaigners ask us to defer without scepticism to the supposed knowledge of medical scientists, macroeconomists and climate scientists, among others, but we usually cannot bring ourselves to. Our reasonable doubts about their reliability make us reluctant to bear the costs that perfect deference is claimed to warrant.

This is not how the behavioural economist Daniel Kahneman interprets our reluctant deference. He thinks that we fail to respond as certified experts and campaigners wish we would because of an evolutionary defect in our brains:

> Let's suppose that the scientific consensus is correct: global warming is happening, and it will have some catastrophic consequences. By the time it becomes obvious to everyone that it's a danger, it will probably be too late to do anything that will be effective in combating it. As a species, our brains have just not evolved to deal with threats whose effects

will be felt in what, for us, counts as the remote future. We respond to them by ignoring them.[5]

He goes on to suggest that climate scientists have failed to convince ordinary people of their claims because they have relied on evidence and arguments rather than trust:

Scientists ... present evidence, figures, tables, arguments, and so on. But that's not how to convince people. People aren't convinced by arguments. They don't believe conclusions because they believe in the arguments that they read in favour of them. They're convinced because they read or hear the conclusions coming from people they trust. You trust someone and you believe what they say. That's how ideas are communicated. The arguments come later ... Why do I believe global warming is happening? The answer isn't that I have gone through all the arguments and analysed the evidence – because I haven't. I believe the experts from the National Academy of Sciences. We all have to rely on experts.[6]

This is the standard view discussed above, with a 'predictable irrationality' twist.[7] Our failure to accept, without scepticism, what climate scientists say is a result of our irrational tendencies. To overcome this, scientists should set aside evidence and argument and instead employ rhetoric that will more effectively

---

5   Interviewed by Alasdair Palmer in 'Mad money', *Spectator*, 28 July 2012.

6   Ibid.

7   According to many psychologists and behavioural economists, human folly is not random but conforms to various patterns. We are predictably irrational. This is almost certainly true. But it does not follow that we are always irrational. There is a tendency in those who have learned some of this behavioural economics to see irrationality everywhere. Yet what they deem irrational behaviour is often merely the result of preferences they have not accounted for or of quite proper reasoning that the behavioural economists themselves have failed to understand.

win our trust. Everyone should be persuaded to share Kahneman's deference to the National Academy of Sciences.

To see the error of this view, suppose that, instead of climatic doom, we were told that astrophysicists had detected a large but far-off comet travelling towards the Earth. They are 95 per cent confident that it will strike the Earth in 25 years. We must act now to develop a missile system or something similar that will destroy the comet or divert its course and avert disaster. I cannot be sure, but my guess is that we would overcome our alleged evolutionary inability to face up to far-off problems. We would get to work on building the required missile system.

The difference between the comet case and the climate case is simply that we have a higher degree of confidence in the predictions of astrophysicists than in the predictions of climate scientists. This is indeed a matter of trust. But the trust is not independent of evidence and argument. We trust physicists because of the remarkable success of physics in making accurate predictions and in building technology. The success of physics is evidence for the credibility of physicists' predictions.

Kahneman is right that laymen must rely on experts. But he is wrong that 'the arguments come later'. The arguments come first, and our deference rightly depends on their success: that is, on their resulting in theories that make accurate predictions. The simple, on/off kind of deference apparently recommended by Kahneman, which takes no heed of sciences' records of success or of the temptations for scientists to overstate their cases, would be far sillier than the variable and sceptical kind of deference that most people exercise. Kahneman may well be right that we are predictably irrational. But when it comes to scientific deference, we are not as irrational as he would like us to be.

Concluding remarks

Those who promote paternalistic policies face an obvious question: namely, why should they occupy the role of parents and the rest of us the role of children? What gives them their 'parental authority'? Appealing to science allows them to give the answer that real parents give their children: 'we know more than you do'. Those who would coerce us into living as they see fit are doing nothing more than giving us the benefit of their superior knowledge. They are Plato's philosopher kings, rebranded for the 21st century. Scientist kings.

It is a bluff – as I hope this monograph has shown by close examination of the errors that pollute supposed paradigms of evidence-based policy. Once these errors are exposed, there is another, simpler way to see that our political parents are bluffing when they claim to be nothing but servants of scientific reasoning.

There are two ways in which your opinions can fail to be scientific. One was made famous by Karl Popper (1959). Your beliefs are unscientific when they are based on a theory that does not make testable predictions. A theory that is consistent with anything that could happen – that would 'fit the facts', no matter what the facts turn out to be – is not scientific. It does not answer to reality. Freudian psychology was such a theory, according to Popper. No matter what someone did – whether he yelled or remained silent, killed himself or led a life of laughter, loved his father or hated him – Freudianism could explain it.

To understand the other way of being unscientific, consider astrology. It is not unscientific in Popper's sense. It makes testable predictions. It says that people born on certain dates have certain observable characteristics, and that certain kinds of things will happen to them when celestial bodies are in certain arrangements. Indeed, astrology has been tested. And it turns out to be false. Your date of birth does not affect your life in the way that astrology says it does (see, for example, Calson, 1985).

Nevertheless, many people still adhere to astrology. They do not care that astrology has been tested and disconfirmed. Indeed, they care so little that they do not even know that this disconfirmation has happened.

That is not how scientists behave. When a scientist's theory is shown to be wrong he either abandons the theory or revises it in a way that avoids the refutation, or he shows that the refutation itself involves an error. In other words, scientists do not simply ignore apparent refutations of their theories.

But evidence-based policymakers do. For example, I am not the first to point out the many shortcomings of the survey-based measure of happiness adopted by the British government. Nor is this the first time I have exposed them (albeit in less detail elsewhere).[8] Yet those who advance the government's happiness agenda do not abandon or revise their theory. Nor have they explained where objections of the kind I make go wrong. And I do not expect them to do so after the publication of this monograph. The same goes for those who promote minimum alcohol prices and bans on smoking in public places. The exposure of apparently serious defects in their reasoning is a matter of no concern to them. They neither defend nor revise their positions. They proceed not in the fashion of physicists or any other genuine scientists but of astrologers. They are astrologer kings.

---

8   See, for example, 'The Good Life with David Cameron', *Wall Street Journal*, 30 November 2010.

REFERENCES

Calson, S. (1985), 'A double-blind test of astrology', *Nature*, 318: 419–25.

CR Consulting (2010), 'Smoking gun: is the smoking ban a major cause of the decline in the British pub?', London: Corporate Responsibility Consulting Ltd.

Dolan, P., R. Layard and R. Metcalfe (2011), *Measuring Subjective Wellbeing for Public Policy: Recommendations on Measures*, Special Paper no. 23, London: Centre for Economic Performance.

Dyson, F. (2004), 'A meeting with Enrico Fermi', *Nature*, 427: 297.

Enstrom, J. E., and G. C. Kabat (2003), 'Environmental tobacco smoke and tobacco related mortality in a prospective study of Californians, 1960–98', *British Medical Journal*, 326: 1057.

EPA (US Environmental Protection Agency) (1992), *Health Effects of Passive Smoking: Lung Cancer and Other Disorders: The Report of the United States Environmental Protection Agency*, Washington, DC: US Environmental Protection Agency.

Garnaut, R. (2008), *The Garnaut Climate Change Review: Final Report*, Port Melbourne: Cambridge University Press.

Hart, H. L. A. (1961), *The Concept of Law*, Oxford: Clarendon Press.

Hawkey, C., J. Rhodes, I. Gilmore and N. Sheron (2011), 'Drugs and harm to society', *The Lancet*, 377(9765): 554.

HM Treasury (2010), *Review of Alcohol Taxation*, London: HM Treasury.

House of Lords Science and Technology Committee (2010), *Second Report: Behaviour Change*.

IPCC (2007), *A Report of Working Group I of the Intergovernmental Panel on Climate Change: A Summary for Policymakers*, Geneva: Intergovernmental Panel on Climate Change.

Lawson, N. (2008), *An Appeal to Reason: A Cool Look at Global Warming*, London: Duckworth.

Layard, R. (2005), *Happiness: Lessons from a New Science*, London: Penguin.

Mill, J. S. (1863), *Utilitarianism*, London: Parker, Son, and Bourn.

NHS Confederation (2010), 'Too much of the hard stuff: what alcohol costs the NHS', *Briefing*, 193, January.

Nordhaus, W. D. (2007), 'A review of the *Stern Review on the Economics of Climate Change*', *Journal of Economic Literature*, 45(3): 686–702.

Nussbaum, M. C. (2000), *Women and Human Development: The Capabilities Approach*, Cambridge: Cambridge University Press.

Olson, M. (2000), *Power and Prosperity: Outgrowing Communist and Capitalist Dictatorships*, New York: Basic Books.

ONS (2012), *First Annual ONS Experimental Well-being Results*, Newport: Office for National Statistics.

Popper, K. (1959), *The Logic of Scientific Discovery*, London: Routledge.

Sen, A. (1999), *Development as Freedom*, Oxford: Oxford University Press.

Skidelsky, R. and E. Skidelsky (2012), *How Much Is Enough? The Love of Money, and the Case for the Good Life*, London: Allen Lane.

Stern, N. (2006), *Stern Review on the Economics of Climate Change*, London: TSO.

Stiglitz, J., A. Sen and J.-P. Fitoussi (2009), *Report by the Commission on the Measurement of Economic Performance and Social Progress*, Paris: Commission on the Measurement of Economic Performance and Social Progress.

University of Sheffield (2008), *Independent Review of Effects of Alcohol Pricing and Promotion: Part B*, Sheffield: University of Sheffield.

University of Sheffield (2009), *Modelling to assess the effectiveness and cost-effectiveness of public health related strategies and interventions to reduce alcohol attributable harm in England using the Sheffield Alcohol Policy Model version 2.0: Report to the NICE Public Health Programme Development Group*, Sheffield: University of Sheffield.

US Department of Health and Human Services (2006), *The Health Consequences of Involuntary Exposure to Tobacco Smoke: A Report of the Surgeon General*, Atlanta, GA: US Department of Health and Human Services, Centers for Disease Control and Prevention, Coordinating Center for Health Promotion, National Center for Chronic Disease Prevention and Health Promotion, Office on Smoking and Health.

Weizman, M. L. (2007), 'Review of the *Stern Review on the Economics of Climate Change*', *Journal of Economic Literature*, 45(3): 703–24.

ABOUT THE IEA

The Institute is a research and educational charity (No. CC 235 351), limited by guarantee. Its mission is to improve understanding of the fundamental institutions of a free society by analysing and expounding the role of markets in solving economic and social problems.

The IEA achieves its mission by:

- a high-quality publishing programme
- conferences, seminars, lectures and other events
- outreach to school and college students
- brokering media introductions and appearances

The IEA, which was established in 1955 by the late Sir Antony Fisher, is an educational charity, not a political organisation. It is independent of any political party or group and does not carry on activities intended to affect support for any political party or candidate in any election or referendum, or at any other time. It is financed by sales of publications, conference fees and voluntary donations.

In addition to its main series of publications the IEA also publishes a termly journal, *Economic Affairs*.

The IEA is aided in its work by a distinguished international Academic Advisory Council and an eminent panel of Honorary Fellows. Together with other academics, they review prospective IEA publications, their comments being passed on anonymously to authors. All IEA papers are therefore subject to the same rigorous independent refereeing process as used by leading academic journals.

IEA publications enjoy widespread classroom use and course adoptions in schools and universities. They are also sold throughout the world and often translated/reprinted.

Since 1974 the IEA has helped to create a worldwide network of 100 similar institutions in over 70 countries. They are all independent but share the IEA's mission.

Views expressed in the IEA's publications are those of the authors, not those of the Institute (which has no corporate view), its Managing Trustees, Academic Advisory Council members or senior staff.

Members of the Institute's Academic Advisory Council, Honorary Fellows, Trustees and Staff are listed on the following page.

The Institute gratefully acknowledges financial support for its publications programme and other work from a generous benefaction by the late Alec and Beryl Warren.

The Institute of Economic Affairs
2 Lord North Street, Westminster, London SW1P 3LB
Tel: 020 7799 8900
Fax: 020 7799 2137
Email: iea@iea.org.uk
Internet: iea.org.uk

Director General & Ralph Harris Fellow   Mark Littlewood

Editorial Director   Professor Philip Booth

Managing Trustees

Chairman: Professor D R Myddelton

Kevin Bell
Robert Boyd
Michael Fisher
Michael Hintze
Professor Patrick Minford

Professor Mark Pennington
Neil Record
Professor Martin Ricketts
Linda Whetstone

Academic Advisory Council

Chairman: Professor Martin Ricketts

Graham Bannock
Dr Roger Bate
Professor Alberto Benegas-Lynch, Jr
Professor Donald J Boudreaux
Professor John Burton
Professor Forrest Capie
Professor Steven N S Cheung
Professor Tim Congdon
Professor N F R Crafts
Professor David de Meza
Professor Kevin Dowd
Professor Richard A Epstein
Nigel Essex
Professor David Greenaway
Dr Ingrid A Gregg
Walter E Grinder
Professor Steve H Hanke
Professor Keith Hartley
Professor David Henderson
Professor Peter M Jackson
Dr Jerry Jordan
Dr Lynne Kiesling
Professor Daniel B Klein
Professor Chandran Kukathas
Professor Stephen C Littlechild

Dr Eileen Marshall
Professor Antonio Martino
Dr John Meadowcroft
Dr Anja Merz
Professor Julian Morris
Professor Alan Morrison
Paul Ormerod
Professor David Parker
Professor Victoria Curzon Price
Professor Colin Robinson
Professor Charles K Rowley
Professor Pascal Salin
Dr Razeen Sally
Professor Pedro Schwartz
Professor J R Shackleton
Jane S Shaw
Professor W Stanley Siebert
Dr Elaine Sternberg
Professor James Tooley
Professor Nicola Tynan
Professor Roland Vaubel
Dr Cento Veljanovski
Professor Lawrence H White
Professor Walter E Williams
Professor Geoffrey E Wood

Honorary Fellows

Professor Michael Beenstock
Sir Samuel Brittan
Professor Ronald H Coase
Professor David Laidler
Professor Chiaki Nishiyama

Professor Sir Alan Peacock
Professor Vernon L Smith
Professor Gordon Tullock
Professor Basil S Yamey

Other papers recently published by the IEA include:

Taxation and Red Tape
The Cost to British Business of Complying with the UK Tax System
Francis Chittenden, Hilary Foster & Brian Sloan
Research Monograph 64; ISBN 978 0 255 36612 0; £12.50

Ludwig von Mises – A Primer
Eamonn Butler
Occasional Paper 143; ISBN 978 0 255 36629 8; £7.50

Does Britain Need a Financial Regulator?
Statutory Regulation, Private Regulation and Financial Markets
Terry Arthur & Philip Booth
Hobart Paper 169; ISBN 978 0 255 36593 2; £12.50

Hayek's *The Constitution of Liberty*
An Account of Its Argument
Eugene F. Miller
Occasional Paper 144; ISBN 978 0 255 36637 3; £12.50

Fair Trade Without the Froth
A Dispassionate Economic Analysis of 'Fair Trade'
Sushil Mohan
Hobart Paper 170; ISBN 978 0 255 36645 8; £10.00

A New Understanding of Poverty
Poverty Measurement and Policy Implications
Kristian Niemietz
Research Monograph 65; ISBN 978 0 255 36638 0; £12.50

The Challenge of Immigration
A Radical Solution
Gary S. Becker
Occasional Paper 145; ISBN 978 0 255 36613 7; £7.50

Sharper Axes, Lower Taxes
Big Steps to a Smaller State
Edited by Philip Booth
Hobart Paperback 38; ISBN 978 0 255 36648 9; £12.50

Self-employment, Small Firms and Enterprise
Peter Urwin
Research Monograph 66; ISBN 978 0 255 36610 6; £12.50

Crises of Governments
The Ongoing Global Financial Crisis and Recession
Robert Barro
Occasional Paper 146; ISBN 978 0 255 36657 1; £7.50

... and the Pursuit of Happiness
Wellbeing and the Role of Government
Edited by Philip Booth
Readings 64; ISBN 978 0 255 36656 4; £12.50

Public Choice – A Primer
Eamonn Butler
Occasional Paper 147; ISBN 978 0 255 36650 2; £10.00

The Profit Motive in Education: Continuing the Revolution
Edited by James B. Stanfield
Readings 65; ISBN 978 0 255 36646 5; £12.50

Which Road Ahead – Government or Market?
Oliver Knipping & Richard Wellings
Hobart Paper 171; ISBN 978 0 255 36619 9; £10.00

The Future of the Commons
Beyond Market Failure and Government Regulation
Elinor Ostrom et al.
Occasional Paper 148; ISBN 978 0 255 36653 3; £10.00

Redefining the Poverty Debate
Why a War on Markets is No Substitute for a War on Poverty
Kristian Niemietz
Research Monograph 67; ISBN 978 0 255 36652 6; £12.50

The Euro – the Beginning, the Middle ... and the End?
Edited by Philip Booth
Hobart Paperback 39; ISBN 978 0 255 36680 9; £12.50

The Shadow Economy
Friedrich Schneider & Colin C. Williams
Hobart Paper 172; ISBN 978 0 255 36674 8; £12.50

Other IEA publications

Comprehensive information on other publications and the wider work of the IEA can be found at www.iea.org.uk. To order any publication please see below.

Personal customers

Orders from personal customers should be directed to the IEA:
Clare Rusbridge
IEA
2 Lord North Street
FREEPOST LON10168
London SW1P 3YZ
Tel: 020 7799 8907. Fax: 020 7799 2137
Email: crusbridge@iea.org.uk

Trade customers

All orders from the book trade should be directed to the IEA's distributor:
Gazelle Book Services Ltd (IEA Orders)
FREEPOST RLYS-EAHU-YSCZ
White Cross Mills
Hightown
Lancaster LA1 4XS
Tel: 01524 68765. Fax: 01524 53232
Email: sales@gazellebooks.co.uk

IEA subscriptions

The IEA also offers a subscription service to its publications. For a single annual payment (currently £42.00 in the UK), subscribers receive every monograph the IEA publishes. For more information please contact:
Clare Rusbridge
Subscriptions
IEA
2 Lord North Street
FREEPOST LON10168
London SW1P 3YZ
Tel: 020 7799 8907. Fax: 020 7799 2137
Email: crusbridge@iea.org.uk